DATE DUE			

RAISING
THE
RAFTERS

RAISING

THE

RAFTERS

How to Work with Architects, Contractors, Subcontractors, Interior Designers, Suppliers, Engineers and Bankers to Get Your Dream House Built

STEPHEN F. COLLIER

THE OVERLOOK PRESS
WOODSTOCK • NEW YORK

First published in 1993 by
The Overlook Press
Lewis Hollow Road
Woodstock, New York 12498

Library of Congress Cataloging-in-Publication Data

  Collier, Stephen F.
    Raising the rafters : how to work with architects, contractors,
    interior designers, subcontractors, suppliers, engineers, and
    bankers to get your house built / Stephen F. Collier.

      p. cm.
    Includes index.
    1. House construction.   I. Title.
TH4811.C59   1993
ISBN : 0-87951-490-6   92-35994
                                      CIP

To Barby,
my wife and loving partner.
Thank you for your patience and assistance
in making this book possible.

Many thanks to Rebecca Chaney,
Joe McIlhaney, Pete Craycroft, Scott Sterling,
Pat and Tina McClellan, William and Kelly Glasgow,
Susan Kay, Scott Stucky, Duncan Butler,
Tom and Marji Delatour and the many others
for reviewing and advising me in this effort.

Special thanks to Bob Kay
whose challenge about priorities started the whole process.

CONTENTS

Introduction

The Architect/Designer—
The Creative Problem Solver

CONTENTS

The Contractor/Builder—
The Experienced Coordinator

Predesign—
The Rules to Dream By

Design—Solving the Problem

Construction Documents— Communicating What to Build and the Quality

Consultants—The Specialists

Bidding and Negotiations— Selecting a Contractor and / or Arriving at the Contract Price

CONTENTS

The Contract for Construction

Financing—The Money to Build It

Construction—Coordinating the Masses, or The Fight of Your Life

CONTENTS

RAISING
THE
RAFTERS

INTRODUCTION

Please read the Introduction!

Welcome to the strange and wonderful world of home design and construction. Nothing can give more satisfaction (and grief) than the conception and construction of your dream house. It can be a roller coaster of emotions when you review design sketches and realize the real cost to build it, when you feel the high of record-breaking construction speeds and the depression of construction problems, all culminating with the move-in and the discovery that the thermostat doesn't turn the heat on. The early settlers had it relatively easy. Homes were built with the wood or stone found near the construction site. Nowadays wood studs are shipped in from Washington, windows from Minnesota, plastic pipes from Texas and garage door-opener microcircuits from across the ocean. Our homes have become complex machines for comfort instead of basic shelter from the elements, and the literally thousands of people involved with your home can hold the key to your happiness. If the plumber's helper places the wrong pipe under the concrete foundation, or the assembly line worker who insulated your windows missed a spot of glue, you will feel the result. But if you do your homework and keep your heart at bay, the whole process can actually be manageable and enjoyable.

I am an architect by training but please don't hold that against me. There are some of us who know how to design artful yet practical homes while holding to a budget. And because I design homes for families, I find I am also part marriage counselor, family planner and arbitrator between contractors, bankers, subcontractors, appraisers and owners. Many architects avoid designing houses for these very reasons. Commercial buildings can be less complicated and the building owners can leave them at work, go home and relax in their personal places—places designed for their emotional well-being by architects like myself. I have enjoyed being associated with all types of projects—from bathroom additions to grand estates, from ski cabins to greenhouses—and I have found, especially with home projects, that you're not just building a home, you're building relationships, relationships that could make or break your project or bank account. The following writings are a product of my experience and the result of pressure from people who found themselves distraught in the middle of the biggest investment of their lives—the construction of their homes.

What is this book about and how do I find my way through it?

Just as home construction begins with selecting the architect or builder and a design—organizing the design into documents (plans, etc.), making it possible to calculate the cost of the home and build it—the following chapters have been organized in this manner. The architect and builder are discussed first, followed by how a home is designed and documents prepared; next are other issues related to the design and construction, then how the cost of the home is determined, how it's financed and constructed and the concerns with moving in and beyond. The final chapter discusses who represents you best at various stages of the project—the architect or the builder. But please don't jump to the end. The beginning chapters lay the foundation for this debate and we all know how important a good foundation is.

Once you begin the whole process, your ideal goals should be to get the home you've imagined, for the price you calculated, at the time you've prepared to move in. These should be the goals of all who serve you—the designer, builder, contractor, sub-contractors, suppliers, bankers, consultants and anyone else. I will try to cover what you should know to meet these goals. It is a question-and-answer format to help you quickly find answers as you need them.

Although the issues and problems mentioned may at times seem extreme, the intention is to make you aware of the possible hazards that await you—not to create a mood of distrust between you and the people you will encounter during the adventure. I hope you will read between the lines that I am an optimist. I normally give people the benefit of the doubt, but time and experience have made me a realist when it comes to managing personalities and money in the building process.

All the issues related to this book are for the design and construction of new houses—not remodeling. Although most of the concepts are similar, a remodeling is a very different animal, filled with issues surrounding the existing structure.

How many decisions are there to make?

Throughout the book I will refer to the thousands of decisions made from the beginning of design to the time you move in to your new home. There are literally thousands of decisions to be made, and luckily you are not involved in every one. Someone will, however, make each of these decisions and every one of them will be made in proper sequence or your house will not be finished. If the electrician's aide puts 150-watt bulbs in lights that will only safely handle 60-watt bulbs, for instance, the house is not complete until they are replaced. You need the most appropriate person to make every decision, for there are possibly thousands of mistakes to be made. A system of review, checks and balances should be set up to minimize them.

As an example of the vast number of decisions to be made, let's talk about your kitchen cabinets. Will they be painted or stained? How high off the floor should the upper shelves be? What material are the doors made of—pine, oak, poplar, soft maple? What is the structure made of? If you paint them, which of the hundreds of colors will you choose? Will the color match the counter tops? What hinges should you use—plain pivot, European double spring, hidden type, heavy-duty, paintable? What doorknob (or pull) will you pick? How much can you spend on door pulls? Some cost five times more than others. Where exactly do you want the pull on the door? Should the drawer-trim details match the doors? Is the space above the upper shelf open or filled with a wall and wallpaper?

Other decisions you will not necessarily be involved with, but which are just as important, are: the moisture content of the wood during framing, the type of nail used to apply the wall studs, the strength of the concrete, the size of the reinforcing steel, how the materials are stored before installation, the gauge of electric wire, the location of the air-conditioning unit to prevent noise in the master bedroom, the location of the plumbing drains to prevent flushing noise in the dining room, etc., etc.

Murphy's Law must have been written for construction: "If anything can go wrong it will." If there were two thousand decisions to be made from the beginning to the end of your project (this is not too far off), what percentage would you expect to be correct? Of course you want them all correct, but there will be some bad decisions made, some that can be corrected and some that cannot. In any business you would expect a certain percentage of problems, and it is no different in the construction field. If only one percent of the decisions were poorly made, that is twenty bad decisions. Make sure they are not important ones. Much is discussed in the following questions about the problems with poor, bad or dishonest decisions—how to guard against them and what to do when they occur.

If you are new to the construction world you may find the number of decisions to make overwhelming. But be calm: most architects or builders can guide you through the timing, importance and prerequisites of every decision. You have plenty of time to do your research and make thoughtful decisions. But be aware, there are many of them.

What kind of guide do I need?

A few years ago, with our three-week vacation approaching, my wife and I decided to go to Europe. We were young and had some extra cash, no children and an itch to go far away, but with the deadline approaching there was little time to plan such a trip. We had never been to any foreign country and looked forward with anticipation to seeing these historic and romantic places. But we were also anxious about the strange customs we were about to encounter. How would we get around in a country where we could not speak the language? How would we order food or find a hotel and, most important, what would we do in case of an emergency?

One of the first things we did was to buy a book about the places we were planning to go. This book informed us what unusual customs we might expect in the various countries, recommended some good restaurants and gave us tips for transportation and language barriers (we made sure we could say "Where is the rest room?" in several languages). The travel book certainly came through for us. We relied on it all the time, and its raveled pages soon became stained with fingerprints. During our travel research we discovered that Italy, one of the places we wanted to visit, had a special one-week tour, including tour guides, hotels and meals at a price we could not refuse. We eventually decided to spend the first two weeks touring on our own and end with the guided tour of Italy.

Once we arrived in Italy and joined our tour, we found guides, drivers and other folks aiding us in our travels and travails. Even though going it alone offered some wonderfully memorable moments, we found that following a guide's advice was much easier. Our tour guide helped us with exchanging currency, speaking the language, telling us rules like not to handle the fruit before purchasing it (the vendor would pick it up for us; we weren't to soil fruit with our fingers). She had been all over Italy exploring places to go and places to avoid. A certain trust grew between us, partly because we needed someone to lean on in this strange territory, and she seemed to be looking out for our best interests.

However, one night after dinner, as we were walking back to our hotel, we observed our guide at the back of the restaurant with our waiter, exchanging some currency. The waiter paid her for bringing us to the restaurant. Our picture of our guide quickly changed. Although she had shown us a wonderful place to eat, was she looking out for us or for herself? Was there another restaurant where we would have had a better, less expensive meal?

The design and construction of your home can be as exciting and tension-filled as traveling to a foreign country. Although you may know the local terrain a little, you can soon find yourself lost in a sea of building jargon, trying to interpret plans and specifications written in a strangely unfamiliar form of English, and dealing with unfamiliar issues between the contractor, designer, suppliers and subcontractors. Whom do you trust when something unexpected goes wrong with one of the biggest cash expenditures of your life? You should do your research, but most important you need an experienced guide, who represents you as much as possible, to help you through the maze.

Who is your best guide? A book? The architect? The builder? How do you select an architect or builder? Should you bid the project among several builders? or choose one at the beginning? What happens when one of the more than two thousand decisions made from the beginning to the end is a wrong one? How do you control the large amount of money flowing from the bank in your name?

The aim of this book is to answer these and many more questions. In it we plan to:

1. help you get familiar with the many issues dealing with the design and construction of your home
2. help you make informed decisions and make you aware of risks associated with the paths you wish to travel during the process
3. give you a head start on selecting the most appropriate guide
4. help you create a system of checks and balances to deal with problems when they arise and, most important, the money as it flows.

The more unfamiliar the territory, the greater the need for a guide. The more complicated the project, the greater the possibility for confusion and/or monetary mismanagement.

THE ARCHITECT/ DESIGNER
The Creative Problem Solver

Where do I find a good residential architect or home designer?

If you are fortunate enough to know an architect or home designer, this question is not very important to you. But if you have just moved to an unfamiliar place or do not care to use a designer you know, finding a good residential architect or home designer can be easier than looking randomly through the phone directory. Believe it or not, I have been surprised by a call from someone who just opened the yellow pages and found my small name among hundreds of architects. This method should be your last resort.

When you find a good mechanic for your car or dentist for your family, you've found someone you can trust with your important possessions. You will constantly need help with your automobiles and teeth, and building a relationship with these people can be comforting. If one of them makes a mistake or treats you unfairly, you can find another relatively easily through friends, relatives or other references. But what about finding a person you will deal with only once, for a short period of your life, who also happens to be a steward of your dreams, money and future home. The selection can be more stressful. The goal is not simply to find any architect or home designer, but to find a good one. You could take the yellow pages route and interview several designers, but there are easier ways.

An AIA (American Institute of Architects) chapter exists in most metropolitan areas. Although not all architects belong to the AIA, many are registered there, and their files show what kind of work they do. Give the AIA a call and ask for architects who do residential design. Not all architects do houses; some do both houses and commercial work, while others specialize in residential design. This will narrow the field and get you to some qualified designers.

Networking through friends and business associates, or calling contractors or building suppliers, could lead you to a few names. Call each architect and designer and ask for referrals, where you could see some of their work and how they charge for their services. Make sure you call some of their references: How did they find this architect to work with? Are they satisfied with the design? Did the project exceed their budget? Thorough answers to these questions are very important.

If you plan to go to the builder first, he can offer several suggestions. The builder might use only one architect, might have one in his office or might even have hired several different designers to design his homes. Ask this architect or designer the same questions mentioned above, as well as whether he will represent you or feel allegiance to the builder if something goes wrong during construction.

What qualities should I look for in an architect/designer?

Both the architect and the home designer combine many different talents and experiences. Each provides a different level of service—some are more experienced, others are exceptionally creative and all have personalities you may or may not relate to. When you are seeking a home designer, you are searching for the best combination of these factors.

The level of training and experience of both the architect and home designer are of utmost importance. A young architectural student who has just returned from foreign travel and makes excellent grades in her senior year may give you a whale of a deal on her design fee, and you may get a whale of a wonderful design, but the construction documents produced (a critical portion of your contract with the builder) may well be lacking if she has not been adequately trained in the practical side of construction techniques. A home designer may have designed hundreds of houses for various builders but may have had limited exposure to the wider world of wonderful design possibilities.

If you have a specific idea of what the house should look like—e.g., a period Williamsburg home or a modern Miesian glass box house—the amount of experience the designer has with that type of work can be important. Although some architects can design on either side of the imagination, most have a preference for a certain design feel or style. Look at their portfolio and photographs of their finished work. Walk through some of their creations, and you can tell where they lean in design. You will be able to tell if this architect will meet your needs. Also, when looking at a designer's work, try to look at it without pigeon-holing him into a certain style. Very few homes have a purist sense about their design. Most are a mixture of modern and classical imagery and have been influenced by the owners who occupy them.

Other important factors in selecting an architect or home designer are their communication skills and personality. During the design process, will the designer listen to your concerns? If he doesn't listen during the interview, but constantly interjects his own desires and opinions, will he listen after you hire him? Many people enjoy a charismatic personality who will make the project an adventure, but few wish to be ignored.

How large is the firm of architects or designers, and who will do the work? If you have a small, inexpensive project and go to a larger design firm (ten people or more), the person lowest on the management ladder may have charge of your project, even if you always speak to the owner at meetings. Ask who will be doing the various stages of the work. You want the person best suited for the job to work on your home. In most cases the owners or more experienced people in the firm will do the design work, and draftsmen or intern architects will do the drafting under their supervision.

Are there different types of architects and designers?

There are as many types of architects and designers as there are needs of the owners they will serve. Some owners enter the market with a very low construction budget and wish to save money by doing some work themselves. They would rather buy a better appliance package than spend that money on planning.

On the other extreme are those who wish to live in a unique or artistically designed home. They too can have a limited budget, but they appreciate the talents of the designers they hire and wish to maximize their gifts. These owners do not care to be too involved in the construction process and want the people they hire to deal with all the troubles of construction while they relax and enjoy the process.

Many other owners fall in between these two extremes, owners who do not have the resources to hire the full services of professionals but still want good design and representation throughout the process. The number of decisions you make with the advice of the architect or designer will help determine the type of designer you choose and how much his or her fee will be.

I like to place design professionals into three categories: the artist architect, the design architect and the home designer. These are general categories, and many architects and designers can provide varying levels of service at different fees. But for the sake of simplicity let's stuff them into these three.

The artist architect is the designer most used by the second person described above. These architects have been written about in magazines and have won design awards. The owner hires them for their artistic talents and pays the top fee for their services. All two thousand decisions are made with the direct input of this designer. He is involved from site selection until you move into your finished home.

Most of this designer's advice is given during the design phase and production of construction documents (plans and specifications; these will be discussed more in the chapter called Construction Documents). Each decision is recorded on the plans and specifications. The size and location of each room is designed as usual, but this person deals with the texture and color of each wall as well as every piece of trim. The heating, ventilation and air-conditioning system (the HVAC system) is designed by an engineer instead of the subcontractor bidding the job. To aid in selecting light fixtures, they have volumes of product literature or will take you to various suppliers. Each part of the house has the designer's touch, making it a unique, unified design.

The plans and specifications (or "specs") prepared by the artist architect are extremely detailed, filled with methods and descriptions of how to execute each piece of the home. The "plans" show where the walls, doors and windows are located; the "elevations" show how the exterior looks, and each detail is drawn to show how the work is put together. The "door schedule," "window schedule" and "room finish schedule" are detailed charts describing each element of the house. The window schedule, for example, describes whether each window is painted or stained, if the panes are double or single glass, if the window is wood or metal and whether it operates as a "double-hung" or a casement. Every interior piece of trim is selected and detailed for the trim carpenter to install. The specifications describe the quality standards required to install every aspect of the work.

On the other end of the design profession is the home designer. This designer is either an architect apprentice who never took or passed the architectural boards or a draftsman trained in home design by a home builder. The home designer will work directly for a single builder or as an independent designer for several builders. When an owner approaches a discount builder first and the builder needs some plans drawn, he typically refers the new clients to a home designer.

The home designer deals with the relationship of rooms, the layouts of the kitchen and baths and the appearance of the exterior, but seldom gets into the details of how to construct them. Often the home designer has a book of different types of plans and elevations similar to those you could find in bookstores. The owners select the plan that most closely meets their needs, and if changes are to be made, the predrawn plans are adjusted accordingly. Construction details are left to the builder, who uses his standard methods of construction. Most of the two thousand construction decisions are made with the advice of the builder—for instance, the interior wall texture, window types, exterior trim details and quality standards.

The documents produced by the home designer are commonly referred to in the business as a "builder's set," or a set of plans and specs that minimally describe what the builder needs to get a building permit and build the home. These show where the walls, doors and windows are located, what the elevations look like and, sometimes, the positioning of cabinet doors and drawers.

The design architect falls in the middle of these two extremes. This person is a registered architect who probably aspires to be an artist architect. He or she would like to command the fees and get the exposure of the artist architect but needs more time or has a more practical approach to design. The owner who still desires a person trained in the construction industry with good design ability but who does not wish to pay the higher fee will use the design architect or a designer who has worked directly with both builders and owners.

This person is used when the owner feels comfortable making some decisions about design without the aid of the designer. Usually one-half to three-fourths of the two thousand decisions are made with the design architect. Room layout, door and window locations and kitchen and bath layouts are determined just as with the home designer, but the design is taken further with consideration of the structure and whether HVAC ducts will come into conflict with any beams. Exterior details are thought out and drawn for the builder, and selection of the exact roofing material is part of the total design of the exterior. These are just a few of the decisions.

Notice that personalities were not mentioned when describing each of the three types of designers. Many people feel that if they select an artist architect they will hire a prima donna who is interested in building a monument to his ego, interested only in publicity and not the satisfaction of his client. They may also think that by selecting the home designer they have chosen a "yes man" willing to do whatever they desire. In fact, both personality extremes are found among home designers, design architects and artist architects. Of course few people have such extreme character traits and most, though they take pride in their work, will be open to other ideas.

How does the architect/designer charge for his services?

This issue can be very confusing when you don't know about the design and construction process. As mentioned earlier, thousands of decisions will be made from the conception of the project to the time you move in. The amount of an architect's or designer's fee is based on the number of decisions you make with his or her advice.

The process of design and construction of your home typically follows the following phases described in detail later in other chapters: predesign, design, bidding and negotiations and construction. The services of the architect and designer follow the same phases. Most people know that the designer draws the plans and writes the specifications, but this only touches the surface of what he can do for you.

Just as I describe three categories of designers above (artist architect, design architect and home designer), I like to break the levels of service into three types: full service, medium service and minimal or builder's service. Typically the artist architect provides a full service. The home designer normally provides a builder's service, can provide the medium service but seldom if ever provides a full service. The design architect can provide all three.

Full service is one in which the architect advises you throughout the whole project—design, construction documents, bidding and negotiations and construction. Full service also means that almost all decisions are made with the advice of the architect—including interior selections and colors as well as all exterior details. The medium service provides aid to you in all phases of the project, similar to a full service, but only about half of the decisions are made with the architect's help. The designer may help with the plans and exterior details but leave the interior design and color selections to you. Minimal or builder's service normally takes place in accord with a builder and deals only with the design and drafting of your plans and elevations. Seldom are exterior or interior details provided. Most of the two thousand decisions are aided by the builder, and the documents provided by this service cannot be competitively bid among different contractors.

FULL-SERVICE FEE

In the classic full service, the architect is the owner's guide and aid throughout the project. He or she will not only design and draw each part of the project, but will also aid and advise you during the bidding phase, help negotiate the contract with the builder, observe the construction to ensure the project is being built according to the contract, approve the monies requested by the builder during construction, hire appropriate consultants (structural, mechanical, electrical, etc.) and help you make the final list of items to be finished before moving into the home. With full service, nearly all two thousand decisions are made with the aid of the architect and recorded in a detailed set of construction documents before bids are taken.

The fee for a full service ranges from 10 to 15% of the construction cost of your home. Suppose, for example, you plan on spending $200,000 for a 3000-square-foot house. If you hired the architect to do a full service, the fee may be 10% of $200,000, or a $20,000 fee. If the construction budget were $100,000 for a 2000-square-foot house, the full service fee could be $10,000.

MEDIUM SERVICE

The medium service differs from full service in that about half of the decisions are made with the aid of the architect, while the remainder are made directly with the builder, suppliers and sub-contractors (subs). Broad design decisions come first from the architect. The floor plan is drawn, as well as the structural framing plan, air-conditioning plan, exterior details, etc. Accordingly, since only half of the decisions are made, only half are recorded in construction documents. Sometimes the medium service will not include some later phases of the project, such as bidding and negotiations or construction observation. If the builder has already been selected and the bidding process is controlled by the contractor, the designer may not be needed.

The fee for a medium service ranges from 5 to 8% of the construction of your home. If you plan on spending $200,000 for a 3000-square-foot house and you hired the architect to do a medium service, the fee may be 5% of $200,000, or a $10,000 fee. If the construction budget were $100,000 for a 2000-square-foot house, the full service fee could be $5000. About half the services are performed at about half the cost.

MINIMAL OR BUILDER'S SERVICE

The builder's service is the minimal service provided by the architect/designer, with the largest role taken by the builder. The architect/designer can aid you in all phases of the work, but usually is delegated to only the first phases of services: the design of the house and the drafting of the construction documents. After he finishes, the builder takes over. Room layouts and elevations are designed, but all details are decided on by the builder or his subs. The construction documents are commonly known as a builder's set of drawings.

The fee for a minimal or builder's service ranges from 2 to 4% of the construction cost of your home. If you plan on spending $200,000 for a 3000-square-foot house and you hired the architect or designer to do a minimal or builder's service, the fee could be 2% of $200,000, or a $4000 fee. If the construction budget were $100,000 for a 2000-square-foot house, the minimal service fee could be $2000. I have seen fees as low as $300 for modification of an existing floor plan. Only the basic drafting services are performed, and no advice is provided on bidding or construction. And since the documents are so minimal, it is not advisable for builders to competitively bid a project with so few decisions made and so many left undecided.

In my experience, I have found that people who have been through the home design and construction process more than once spend more the second or third time for architectural aid than the first time. They also invest more money for an architect's help during the construction phase, when most of their money is being spent and the possibilities for problems or deceit is greatest.

Are there alternatives to percentage fees billed by architects and designers?

Many owners will prefer not to pay a fixed design fee based on their final construction bid cost. They feel this method motivates the designer to try to raise the project's construction cost in order to raise his own fee. They also may feel that the designer should not get a higher fee simply because the owner decides to use a more expensive material, such as marble flooring instead of vinyl. Both of these conflicting motives can be removed by having the designer fix his fee based on the original estimated construction cost instead of the final outcome of bids. The fee would remain the same no matter what material is chosen for the flooring, and the designer would get no extra money if the project grew more expensive.

There are other ways designers and architects bill for their services. I mentioned the fixed fee first as a means of describing the levels of service of an architect or designer. Although there are other billing methods for design services, the total fee will normally equal the total amount of the fixed fee for the various levels of service. The difference is the incentives or motives created by the optional billing methods. A couple of other ways you could be billed for design services are hourly or by the square foot of construction.

HOURLY BASIS ALTERNATIVE BILLING METHOD

Many architects will bill on an hourly basis for all or some of the work they perform, or will bill a combination of hourly for some phases of work and a fixed fee for others. In most cases the hourly fee is billed for work when duration of a task is difficult to determine.

One reason for billing hourly is that the owner could save some money if the design phase goes by quickly, if decisions are made thoughtfully and thoroughly and the work is done efficiently. The architect is also assured he will not lose money if the design phase takes longer than estimated.

The length of time is more easily estimated for the construction documents and bidding and negotiations phases. The architect can easily estimate the number of drawings he needs to draft and how long each will take. Bidding/negotiations and construction observation also take a more easily estimated amount of time and can be billed either hourly or on a fixed-fee basis. When work is done hourly, seldom will the total fee exceed that of the fixed fee.

SQUARE-FOOT BASIS

Similarly when a designer bills on a square-foot basis, the fees seldom differ from the fixed-fee amounts; the square-foot fee is only a different way of describing the same fee. If the designer were to perform a builder's service and bill the whole job on a square-foot basis, the fee you could expect on the previous example would be $2000, or $0.66 per square foot for the 3000-square-foot house. A medium service would cost $1.66 per square foot, or $5000 for the same 3000-square-foot home. The area determines the square-foot fee and usually includes only the air-conditioned/heated portion of the house, not the area of garages or porches.

Why do some architects/designers charge more than others?

Obviously the full service would take more time and cost more money than a medium service, even if provided by the same firm. But why would one architect who provides the same service charge more or less than another?

What architects and designers charge for their services is a combination of their office overhead, the efficiency of their firm, the profit they desire and what they think they are worth relative to other professionals. If the firm is housed downtown in a very prestigious skyscraper, you could assume their office rent is high. If they have many employees and benefits for those employees, someone must pay for these, and all these factors are likely to be calculated into the fee you pay for their work.

Efficiency is an unusual word when speaking of a design firm. We think of an engine running efficiently when it does a lot of work using little fuel, but how does that relate to a design office?

The efficiency of an office is defined by the amount of work employees do that is billable work, versus nonbillable, and how quickly those employees do the billable work. Some firms have employees that are both skilled and quick; other's don't. Efficient firms can provide you with the same service at a lower cost.

How much profit an architectural or design firm earns and what its owners think they are worth are vague and complex issues. Each firm has its own way of determining these values. Many will simply take the amount they pay their employees, add a factor for office overhead and add a profit factor on top. Other firms will look around the city to learn what other designers are charging and charge the same, hoping their overhead is not too high. By looking at all these factors—the size of the firm, its location, its overhead, the efficiency of its employees and so forth—you can see why some firms can charge less than others for the same service.

What is the difference between an architect and a home designer?

Vitruvius, a first-century architect said,

The architect should be equipped with the knowledge and understanding of different branches of learning as required to judge the quality of artistic work. Architects who have many manual skills and dexterity without scholarship are not able to reach the professional heights which their position warrants. Those with scholarship and no practical skill hunt the shadow not the substance of those who have the thorough knowledge of both practice and theory and a position to obtain and wield authority.

Vitruvius had in mind the difference between what is now a registered architect and a home designer. Although both the architect and home designer can provide a wonderfully designed home, there is a difference between the two. Both can have varying levels of artistic talent and similar levels of experience with construction work. What distinguishes them is their training. The home designer may work more often with builders, providing more minimal sets of construction documents. An architect may work more often with the owners and general contractors, providing more detailed drawings. Both can provide differing levels of service. You must meet each one and see his work to decide which best suits you, but the difference between the two will largely be formal or informal training, in or out of school.

The education of a home designer may range from simple drafting classes in high school to a degree in architecture from a major university. Many home designers have been trained by the builders they work for, and though they have a good grasp of drafting techniques, many have never been trained in design, engineering or other related areas. Others with architecture degrees are trained in design and engineering, but haven't taken, or have failed to pass, the testing boards to become a registered architect.

Few people know it is illegal to call yourself an architect unless you have passed exams provided by the state certification board. However, seldom does designing a residence break these limits to practicing architecture. A paralegal can give legal advice, nurses can aid in the treatment of illnesses, and a bookkeeper can do your accounting; but there is a line that keeps people from giving advice they are not trained to give. They might not be familiar with the big professional picture or the details of a problem and might do more harm than good. The professional was formally trained in the history, philosophy and concepts of his or her profession. Formal training means unlearning what the student thinks he should do, retraining him in correct methods and testing him to determine that he knows the details and practical aspects of what he will practice.

Most architectural schools require five or six years to receive a degree. It really does take a couple of years for a new student to unlearn what he thinks an architect is supposed to do and then learn creative problem solving and visual communication. Training includes designing several types of projects; structural, mechanical, electrical, plumbing and acoustical engineering; legal and professional practice procedures; and visual communication such as drawing, model making or computer-aided design and drafting (CADD).

Once the architectural student receives the degree, his training does not end. The intern architect must go through three or more years of apprenticeship, completing requirements in different areas of architecture. Only then will he be qualified to take the state exam. The architectural registration exam is a two-to-three-day ordeal testing every area of the architectural profession. Approximately 30% or fewer pass the exam and become legally registered architects.

One other factor that may help you choose between an architect and a home designer involves who pays their fees, and who represents you best during construction. In general, a home designer is referred to you by the builder and is paid by the builder. And even though some home designers may act independently from builders, the architect is more often in this role.

Doesn't an architect make the project more expensive?

Are some homes more expensive because an architect designed them? Or do architects just work on expensive projects? Unfortunately, sometimes both are true. It is a strange phenomenon that when a builder or subcontractor sees a set of detailed plans and specifications signed by an architect, the construction price sometimes goes up, even if the plans and specifications just outline in more detail the same work the builder or subcontractor would normally do for less money.

The biggest reason a project increases in cost as a result of an architect's inclusion is that construction documents become more detailed. When the plans and specifications get longer and more detailed, a less experienced builder or subcontractor adds a small amount to his bid because he is afraid he'll miss something in the voluminous plans, or he may feel that since the plans and specs are so detailed, the owners will be more demanding about the quality of his work. When either of these factors enters into the builder's or subcontractor's psyche, the price goes up.

Most people in the construction field have worked with an architect at some time; a builder who has had difficulty with architects will probably charge an extra "hassle" fee for working with them, while builders with good working relationships ignore the issue and add no extra fee.

Why not competitively bid among architects and designers?

Suppose you had a basket of apples to sell. If you wanted several people to bid on or give you their best price for the basket of apples, all you would need to do is show each bidder the apples, and they could give you a price. The apples are measurable, in that they can be counted. Even in the more abstract world of construction, if you draw a set of plans that measures the amount of work to be done and write a set of specifications that describe the type and quality of work, you can also get a good price or bid. The scope of the work should be both understandable and measurable.

How does one measure the ability to design a wonderful home? Often the abstract reality of artistic talent can enter the architect selection picture. If all factors are equal—the ability of the architect to satisfy your design needs, the training and experience of the designer, the ease in which you relate personally with each architect and the type and amount of design service—you could have the designers or architects bid against one another. However, there is the aspect of style—of personal preference—to be taken into account. You want the best combination of talent, training, experience, service, personality—and shared sense of design—at the lowest cost.

What Is the AIA?

The AIA (American Institute of Architects) is the professional association for architects. Just as the AMA (American Medical Association) represents physicians and the NAHB (National Association of Home Builders) represents home builders, the AIA is the organization that represents the concerns of the architect.

A misconception about the AIA is that having these letters after a person's name means the person is a registered architect, when in fact it just means that the person is a member of the association. A registered architect is not required to be a member of the AIA, though it is encouraged. Only a portion of all registered architects are members of the AIA, but membership can offer many opportunities for continuing education and advancement.

How do I inform architects or designers that they were not selected?

It is difficult to call someone to relay bad news. Few people have the management skills to do it comfortably, but it should be done and, believe it or not, most professionals would prefer to get these calls than wait for a response. They have been in business for a long time and do not get every project they interview for. In fact most architects will have some questions for you. Their purpose is not to continue to try for the job but to learn how they were perceived by you during an interview and see how they can improve. So be ready for some questions.

When there is a clear objective reason for choosing another architect or designer, your call can be easy. The other firm could do the work in two weeks instead of six, or the other firm had much more experience with this particular type of construction. But seldom are the reasons for choosing an architect so concrete. There may just be a comfort level you have while communicating with the other architect, or there may be a combination of many factors that are hard to describe. And when these subjective issues are the reasoning behind your choice, you can always say, "I just felt more comfortable with the other person." When you call, be open and honest; it will be appreciated more than you think.

THE CONTRACTOR/ BUILDER
The Experienced Coordinator

Where do I find a good builder or contractor?

If you have gone to an architect or home designer and plan to bid your project among several builders, he will give you plenty of qualified builders to choose from. But what if you are starting with no knowledge of who should build your home and have no architects to guide you? As with looking for an architect or home designer, there are better ways than going to the phone book.

The best referrals come from friends or acquaintances who have recently built a home. Get some names and call each, asking them for referrals, where you can see some of their work and how they prefer to charge for their services. You need not ask them how much they would charge to build your home because they do not know what you wish to build. After an in-depth conversation about what you plan to build, they may be able to give you a range of construction costs, but if they are wise they refrain until seeing plans and specifications. Beware of a builder who gives you a price without thorough knowledge of the details of your design. Most good contractors will wait to see your plans and specifications, or have a long discussion about your project, before even mentioning construction cost.

Many contractors and builders are members of various builders' organizations such as the NAHB (National Association of Home Builders). By calling an organization such as this, you can narrow your choices. Ask for those members who specialize in your size or type of home, and then thoroughly investigate their references.

What qualities should I look for in a contractor or builder?

Just like the architect and designer, a contractor and builder are a compilation of many facets. Each provides different levels of service. Some are more experienced. Others have exceptional management skills. And all have different personalities.

The level of training and experience of contractors or builders varies widely. Some grew up in a family of construction workers, learned the trade over the years and eventually became independent builders as an extension of a family tradition. Others have been trained in different fields, possibly receiving other professional degrees, but entered the building field because they saw a good opportunity to make money in the construction market. Even though degrees are available in construction, only a few residential builders have received formal training at a university in that area.

If you have a certain idea of what your house should look like—e.g., a period Georgian home or a post-modern, neoclassic cottage—the level of experience the builder has with that type of work can be important. Is he used to building extremely complicated curved walls? Has he built seven-step crown molding? Has he worked with an architecturally detailed set of construction documents or only builder's sets?

Other important factors in selecting a contractor/builder are his communication style, management skills and personality. Is he used to communicating directly with an owner or working through an architect? Will he have a tendency to take over the project after it is under construction, ignoring the owner's and designer's concerns, or does he seek advice and input from these important people? The contractor/builder needs the management skills to get the job done on time, to motivate his subcontractors to do their work correctly, to correct poorly done work and to pay attention to details of fabricating all components of the house.

As you should for any person you hire for your project, call the references they give you. Ask about how easy the builder was to work with. Did he complete the project on time and within budget? Did he listen to the owner's concerns and, most important, do something about them? Did he return calls promptly? You should be satisfied with these answers before hiring the builder.

How large is the firm of the contractor/builder, and who will actually do the work? When you go to a larger firm, will the person you initially meet actually supervise the construction work? Will they use a superintendent on the job? You should meet the project superintendent and get a sense of what he is like—you will deal a lot with this person. Has this person acted as a superintendent on several other projects or was he just promoted from head framer with your project as his first crack at supervision? He may well be qualified for your small project, but you should take precautions if using a rookie on an expensive project.

Are there different types of contractors/builders?

During the Middle Ages, the secrets of the construction trades were held closely by groups of men in what were called "guilds." Craft guilds were formed to provide training for apprentices, for advancement of construction knowledge and as insurance of quality construction. Most houses for common people were built of nearby wood with a thatched roof. Cloth coverings or wood shutters were used to cover the window openings. Glass was an expensive commodity. Many owners of glass windows would have them removed while on a journey to keep them safe. Grand buildings—churches, palaces—were built by stonemasons, and you can imagine how few palaces and churches there were built in proportion to the number of people needing houses. Masons of the masonry guilds were therefore prone to move from town to town, building to building, wherever a major project was underway. Many masonry buildings took several decades to build. Some cathedrals took several centuries, and grandsons of grandsons worked on the same building. Woodworkers, joiners, thatchers, painters and plasterers were more localized and kept near a town, where they did all available work. Without belonging to a guild, a worker could not easily leave one town and find construction work in another.

Obviously the construction world has changed. Technology, advancement in material science, the education of the common man, union/non-union labor and training, mass-media advertising and overnight air cargo have made the construction world a different place. Builders are quite a different people from what they were even twenty years ago.

I like to categorize modern-day residential builders and contractors as such: mass builders, discount builders, custom contractors and small contractors. As mentioned later in another question, I perceive a difference between what I call a builder and a contractor. Builders normally are in control of the whole process from beginning to end, while contractors are a part of the owner-architect team.

The mass builder builds large subdivisions with relatively small, inexpensive homes. These subdivisions have four or five floor plans designed, with each plan having two or more alternative exterior elevations. These houses are built in rows, many at a time. The slab is poured on the first house one week, and while the slab is being poured on the second, the rough framing work is done on the first. All the work is done in this synchronized order, and few changes to the plans are allowed to maximize efficiency and minimize cost. Because the mass builder builds in such large volume and his emphasis is on efficiency with minimal potential for changes, the costs of his homes are relatively low. Mass builders never competitively bid among other mass builders for individual projects.

The discount builder is a step up in service from the mass builder in that he builds homes one at a time (not in rows) and has a large array of plans to choose from. He will also have a plan designed specifically for a client if needed. He does enough volume to get some special discounts from suppliers and subcontractors and pass those savings on to you. And since he does several jobs at a time, he must hire more staff and superintendents to coordinate the jobs than the custom contractor, and this extra amount of overhead and efficiency management can add some cost to a project. Seldom will discount builders bid for projects.

The custom contractor's office is owned by one or two people who still have their hands directly in the construction. They typically limit the amount of projects they do, since they prefer to stay in control; too many jobs pull them in too many directions. Their small staff and efficient organization can save money, but the amount of time they spend with the owner, subs and suppliers makes them more suited for larger, more complicated jobs. They can work directly with an architect or designer and will bid for more than half of their projects.

The small contractor is similar to the custom contractor and usually aspires to be one. He has a similar service mentality but lacks experience doing larger work and may have trouble getting work because of this. He does some of the hands-on construction work himself, not merely delegating the work to subcontractors and overseeing their efforts. If he can survive, in a matter of time he will become one of the three contractor types mentioned above. He has a good place in the construction industry in that he can do smaller remodeling jobs (between $2000 and $30,000) that many custom contractors will not pursue. This person will bid any project he is allowed to.

How do contractors/builders charge for their services?

There are two ways a builder will charge to coordinate or actually build all or portions of your home. He will either charge a flat fee for the work designated in the construction documents, or will vary his rate depending on the amount of risk involved based on a maximum construction cost. Both of these methods of compensation are discussed in detail in the chapter on contracts.

Why do some builders or contractors charge more than others?

The organization, experience and size of a contractor's office and staff can affect the contractor's/builder's fee and the price of your house. As an example of what affects a builder's fee, think of the builder's office as a retail store. Some stores try to sell in high volume with minimal personal service (such as warehouse stores) and pass the savings on to you. Other, smaller stores sell their goods with an emphasis placed on customer service. The customer of this store is willing to pay for the personal service and quality of merchandise. Builders (or architects, or suppliers) can organize their offices in similar manners depending on the type of work they desire to do—from high-volume / lower-service / lower-fee to low-volume / higher-service / higher-fee.

What is the difference between a builder and a contractor?

In reality there is no legal or formal difference between the builder and the contractor. Both take your design and fabricate it into a livable place. The difference I draw is one of professional perspective and attitude. The perspective and attitude of a builder is different from that of a contractor.

A builder normally is in charge of a project from beginning to end. He is the person an owner first comes to before the designer. He hires the staff, coordinates the design and builds the house. This person has created a methodology of coordinating his work and will continue in this manner if possible. If there is a problem at any point in the process, the builder takes charge and solves it. He can have trouble making the transition to contractor, which requires more of a service- or team-oriented personality. Very seldom will the builder competitively bid for work.

Although the contractor can take a project from the beginning to the end and coordinate designers and other professionals, usually he does not. This person works as a team member, understanding his role and that of the architect and owner. He can even be a little uncomfortable running the whole project, because he realizes his limitations and the need for other professionals and has developed a good relationship with other architects or designers. When problems arise, he will probably call in all parties involved to discuss and solve them. Although he would prefer to be selected up front and not competitively bid for work, he gets much of his work from bidding.

The size, type and cost of your project will affect which of these professionals you should use.

How do I inform contractors or builders that they were not selected?

At some point you will have to choose only one builder or contractor to build your home, and if you interviewed several, the others should be informed of your decision.

If you have bid among several builders using an architect as your aide, the architect can inform them for you. This is the way it is normally done in a bidding procedure. You and the architect look over the bids, and select the contractor you wish to use (not always the lowest bidder) and the architect informs all the bidders for you.

If you do not use an architect or designer in the bidding process or eliminate the bidding process altogether, informing contractors can still be done with less stress than when notifying an architect or designer. There are usually more concrete factors involved in the selection of a contractor than of a designer—namely, the cost of the project or the contractor's experience. It is much easier to tell a contractor that you prefer to work with another because one will do the same work for less money or has done more of this type of work.

However, there are many times the more expensive contractor is preferred over another, making the rejection more difficult. Like most professionals, contractors prefer to be informed by you. They have been in business for a long time and do not get every project they bid. When you call, be open and honest; it is much appreciated.

PREDESIGN

The Rules to Dream By

What is predesign?

Suppose someone came to you and asked you to design a new chair. What would you do first? Would you run off to your studio and spend hours drawing and planning, to come up with what you thought was the essence of the "chair"? Imagine that after you finish, you meet with the client to explain your wonderful leather lounge chair only to find he wanted a handcrafted wooden stool. Better communication up front in the phase called predesign would have avoided this embarrassing situation.

Predesign is the fact-finding part of design. In this phase one tries not to do any design work; it's too early. This is the problem-*seeking* phase, not the time for problem solving or design. One seeks problems to solve. Requesting more square footage than your budget allows is a problem that should be addressed up front. A mistake made in the design of many products is starting design without a clearly defined project.

Issues and information should be brought to the architect/designer until he is overloaded. The information is best presented in a written form and organized for easy referral. List names and ages of persons who will live in the residence, lifestyle issues such as room layouts for frequent entertainment of large groups, numbers and types of appliances to be placed in the kitchen, when you must move into the house, the maximum cost of the project and so on.

Some designers prefer not to see photographs or images you have kept for the interior or exterior, because these may limit or hinder their creative work. Discuss this with the designer before approaching them with photos. Hindering the creative process with photographs is not a typical problem, however; most architects are eager to understand what image you want to achieve. Either way, discuss all information with the designer before design is actually begun.

Three major issues that need to be discussed and balanced during predesign are the budget, quality, and size of your project.

The budget is the amount you want the project to cost. The total budget normally includes the architect's fee, financing and closing costs, new furniture, window coverings, and miscellaneous expenses. By quickly going over the various costs of a project, one can arrive at an anticipated construction budget.

The quality of the project can be described by photographs, descriptions of exterior and interior finishes, information concerning equipment and appliances, referring to comparable projects, and other means.

The size of the project needs to be weighed in relation to the quality and budget. Are there some minimal sizes of rooms? Can some rooms be combined to save square footage? Make a list of rooms you anticipate using, and mention something about their use and relationship to each other. Should the master bedroom be as far away as possible from the children's bedrooms or as close as possible to an infant's room?

These three issues—budget, size and quality—must be balanced and prioritized for an architect to serve you best. One of the three will normally dictate or dominate the others. If the maximum cost of the project is $30,000 and the minimum square footage is 1000 square feet, then certain limits are placed on the quality of the project, because little can be done for $30 per square foot. In most cases there is a limit to the owner's budget, while the quality and size of the project are adjustable. However, sometimes an owner requires a certain size and specific quality. In this situation the budget becomes the low priority and will be adjusted to meet the other standards of the home. Your priorities should play a big part in the design.

During this fact-finding time, the owner should provide copies of the site plan, deed restrictions and other property-related information. A survey of the property, including tree locations, can be helpful but is not always required. Solar angles, street access to the site and building setbacks are more examples of predesign information.

After completion of the predesign phase, you will have a clearly defined set of "Rules to Dream By." You can dream during the design phase, but you must dream by the rules. Although your dream home is over 8000 square feet, the rules may dictate a maximum of 3000 square feet for the budget and quality you desire.

What are deed restrictions?

Have you ever had any concern that someone would build an odorous pig farm next door to your newly constructed house, or that a mechanic would build next door and work on old cars in the front yard? Deed restrictions are the guarantee that these problems will not occur.

Deed restrictions are community arrangements guarding the interests of your immediate neighborhood. These covenants restrict what one can do on one's property to an even greater degree than city building codes and zoning ordinances. The main intent of these restrictions is to preserve the quality of life of the neighborhood. Many are written to preserve property values, and many can even be made on the whim of your property's developer. A typical deed restriction requires your project to have 75% masonry on the exterior. An even more restrictive covenant could be that all homes must have a minimum size of 3500 air-conditioned square feet.

These restrictions are not enforced by city officials but by a person or board who will review your plans and specifications for conformance before allowing you to build on the property.

Not all properties have deed restrictions, and many neighborhoods are so old that the control board no longer exists. But the restrictions still are enforceable. Deed restrictions for your neighborhood should have been made available to you before you purchased your property, but in case you have no record of them, a copy is usually kept at the local county courthouse or where legal records are filed. Ask your builder or architect where to find these.

What are building codes and zoning ordinances and how do they affect my project?

In seventeenth-century London, most of the houses were built of wood and their roofs were thatch. The great fire of 1666 leveled most of these houses. Laws were soon passed requiring that houses be built of brick or stone, and the roofs be made of lead or other materials to reduce the spread of fire from one building to another. This was one of the beginnings of today's building inspection departments. The whole town would be safer if certain regulations were passed and adhered to. By 1740, building departments were created to review construction and make bylaws. Buildings were even divided into types to regulate their construction and the safety of their neighbors. The maximum height of buildings was set at eighty feet, the highest an escape ladder could reach, and wood fireplace hearths were outlawed.

Today, building codes and zoning ordinances protect individual homes and communities from tragedy. The building codes (e.g., Uniform Building Code; National Building Code; Uniform Plumbing Code etc.) are specifically written to provide a minimum standard that will keep the owner or public from harm. These building codes restrict the kinds of pipe that can be used for drinking water to avoid disease, dictate how large wooden floor joists should be to avoid structural failure, and define the number of exit stairs required from a second floor or how wide stairs should be in case of fire, for example.

The zoning ordinance addresses concerns of local communities, such as density of housing or whether a skyscraper could be built across the street from your home. It also tells how much of your property can be covered with roof or pavings, so enough rain-absorbing soil remains to prevent flooding. It keeps the strip-tease shows and bars along certain areas of town and away from your house.

If I provide incorrect information to the architect, designer or builder, who is responsible?

When the architect, designer, builder or any other person receives some information from you or someone under your authority, he should rely on that information to be true and correct. If it is not and he bases his work on it, the fault may lie with you.

Many times the architect will request information about your property before starting design. He may require a copy of deed restrictions, a survey of the property, a contour plan showing how the land drops from one end of the site to the other or a tree survey showing the exact location of trees to be protected. It is reasonable that if the designer designs your home around a certain tree, and the survey shows it in the wrong place, the fault lies not with the designer but with the survey. Unfortunately no one will know that the tree was misplaced until construction has begun and the builder finds the problem. When providing materials to your designers and builders, do not cut corners. You may not know there is a problem until months later.

DESIGN
Solving the Problem

How does an architect sort through information overload? What is design?

Have you ever been overloaded with too much information, and had to sort through it quickly and make a judgment or decision? What if the decision also had to be creative, or unique? Designers deal with this all the time, and architects are formally trained and tested on this—the sorting through and prioritizing of information based on some rules and the creation of a pleasing design. Armed with predesign information, or "the rules to dream by," the architect can start the design process. Several "schemes" can be created to meet the requirements of the rules. Many architects call the design phase "schematic design" for this reason.

Some parts of the design may be dictated by the site. There may be only one relatively flat portion of the lot to build upon, while the rest is vertical cliffs. The flat portion of the lot may be the preferred area to build upon because building on the cliff can

☐ **5 7**

be cost-prohibitive. But most schemes can go in many directions, and every designer could come up with a different scheme. This is where the architect really earns his money. He is trained to sort through the predesign data, distill the information into its basic elements and come up with a scheme to solve the pre-design problem within the rules.

Normally during the design process, the architect will go back to his studio and spend several hours weeding through the predesign information. By your next meeting, some issues will surface and some problems will be solved, but seldom will a final design be created. Good design can take several meetings, getting to know how you feel about certain issues or trying to explain a difficult concept.

Why not buy a set of plans from a magazine or plan book? Isn't it easier to modify an existing plan?

Bookstores and grocery-store magazine racks are full of house plans of every shape and size. Many builders and home designers also have a book of plans they use when designing a new home. But very few plans meet the specific needs of each owner; they must be modified. Rooms need to be larger or the elevations changed in some way. Using a plan book to select a design, however, can be very cost-effective because you are not paying someone to design from scratch.

Although this can be an excellent method to find a house plan, there are several issues that should be discussed before taking this less expensive road. How much can you change a plan without compromising the design? At what point is it easier to start from scratch than to rearrange a plan? Has the plan actually been built before or was it designed for another part of the country? Will the foundation design fit the site you have?

If you find a plan in a book that very closely matches your desires for a house, you have saved a lot of time communicating to a designer, architect or builder what you want. But when you start moving walls around, more things are affected than the walls. The placement of windows on the exterior, the air-conditioning vents and chases or the structural loading of the home may have to change. Someone will have to record each change and the ramifications of the change on a new set of construction documents (plans and specifications).

In my experience with adapting existing plans, if you would need to move more than one quarter of the walls on the plan, you are is essence remodeling the home before it is built and should instead start from scratch. When the designer makes changes to a plan, it can take more time to adjust it (erase the portion of the work being changed, look for problems associated with those changes, solve those problems, redraft the plan) than to start all over. Of course computer-aided drafting makes this process more efficient, but still much work is redone. With a great deal of changes, it can be more difficult for a designer to design around an existing plan than to begin with a blank sheet of paper.

Be cautious when purchasing mail-order plans. Most were designed for a different part of the country and may not meet local building codes. Many have never been built and may have big design problems. I have seen some plans where the headroom above a stair was only five feet. I recommend using magazine plans only as a guide for your architect to show what room layout you prefer or the elevations you desire.

How long will it take to design my house?

When I was a young architect's apprentice, I worked next door to an engineer's office. I had the great idea of purchasing old homes in run-down neighborhoods, those that were surrounded by trees and could not be moved in pieces, and lifting them by helicopter to a site prepared for them. I would make millions. I did not know how much a house weighed, however, and was researching what kind of helicopter could lift such a house. I went next door to the engineer's office, stuck my head in and asked, "How much does a house weigh?" A legitimate question, I thought. After I received a few blank stares, someone asked, "How big a house?" Of course many things affect the weight of a house—especially how big it is.

Depending on the size of your home, the challenge of the site, the complexity of your desires and the amount of work the architect or designer has at the time, the design of your home can take from one week to several months. If you order a plan from a plan book, it takes as long as the post office takes to deliver the plans. When a draftsman is adjusting a plan from a plan book you could expect the design to be finished in one or two weeks. In larger, more complex homes, where an architect is trying to create a detailed composition, the design can take from two weeks to two months or more before the construction documents are started. Discuss with your designer how much time he expects to take for the design phase.

How do I keep track of cost during design?

As the architect or designer goes through the design process, he should stop at various stages to check square footage and review the possible construction cost. If a good attempt is made to review costs up front during design, you can guard against bad news later, after bidding.

An experienced designer who has been involved with constructing similar projects can take the square footage of your home and multiply it by a conservative cost per square foot. The designer can take the comparable square-footage cost, adjust it by the cost of any special items you may have in your design and give a good estimate of construction cost. For example, your architect may have just finished a project that cost $70 per square foot. Because your design is so similar, he can assume your project will cost about the same. If your home is to be 3000 square feet, he can reasonably deduce your home will cost $210,000 (3000 square feet times $70 per square foot).

Another way to get preliminary estimates is to bring in a builder or contractor who will eventually bid the project. This individual can take preliminary designs and use his greater knowledge of the construction marketplace to determine a good estimate.

The only way to know exactly how much your house will cost is to go through the bidding process. Until that begins, any estimate of construction cost is just that—an estimate. The market changes daily, with varying material costs and labor availability, and these factors are the major costs of constructing your home.

How can I avoid disappointment with the completed project?

Have you ever had an idea of how to build something, tried to explain it to someone else by drawing it on a piece of paper, had him or her build it and realized how different it looks on paper from how it looks in reality? The design and construction process can be very confusing if you are not used to visualizing plans and elevations. During your meetings with the designer or architect, every effort should be made to have you understand the design ideas, the floor plan layouts, relationships of rooms, the spaces and the way those spaces look and feel. It is important that you ask questions and request various visual aids discussed below. Make sure you get a good idea of what the designer is showing you before giving your okay to a design. It is a sickening feeling to walk through a finished project that is not what you imagined.

The architect can aid you in many ways in visualizing your home. The floor plan is the best way to show the relationships of spaces. Looking at a plan offers a bird's-eye view of your house without a roof. With the plan you can see how close spaces are to each other, or how long it will take to walk between various rooms. You can anticipate when there will be noise problems with having the children's playroom next to the headboard of your bed.

Elevations of the house, or of a room's interior, can be more difficult to visualize than layout; although they seem three-dimensional, they are not. In elevations, faraway areas are brought to the forefront and perception of depth disappears. A good designer can provide shading on an elevation drawing that will add a sense of depth.

Another method of visualizing elevations or other spaces is by use of three-dimensional sketches. Only a perceptive designer can aid you with this technique. These sketches give a feel for being inside or walking around the design.

Models also make good visualization tools. These can take the form of detailed, correctly colored models, showing exact exterior and interior finishes, or single-color sketch models, showing only the wall and roof forms. The time to make these differs depending on the model, which costs from $100 to $1000 or more. Computer models are another splendid method of viewing your project before construction begins.

Looking at photographs or visiting existing sites or structures that are similar to your space can be an exceptional visualization tool. However, finding a space or project similar to yours may be difficult.

What is my role during the design process?

Your role during the design phase is to be very honest and vocal about your feelings. Be inquisitive. Can you visualize the rooms or elevations? Should the architect make some special sketches? Do not be shy to ask any question during this process. Make sure you understand the design completely.

The architect has gone through several years of schooling and professional apprenticeship. You will not hurt anyone's feelings by saying, "I don't like the way . . ." Let the designer learn from your questions. He may not understand your feelings about certain issues, or you may not understand the design. Let ideas incubate. Make thoughtful decisions. Once the design phase is over, decisions can be very difficult to change.

CONSTRUCTION DOCUMENTS

Communicating What to Build and the Quality

What are construction documents?

From time to time you will hear the architect or contractor refer to the CD's, or construction documents. The construction documents are every written or printed item used as an agreement between you and the contractor. Typically construction documents include the contract for construction between you and the contractor; the plans drawn by the designer, which define the quantities of the project; the specifications prepared by the designer or builder, which define the quality of the project; and any other written or printed agreement made by you and the contractor.

It is important to note that the plans and specifications are part of the contract and should be adhered to just as any part of the contract should. Many people think plans and specs are documents that roughly show requirements to build the project. In fact they are the *only* reference to the quantities, locations and quality of the project. When a dispute arises about what the contractor is required to do, these documents will clarify matters. Anything not written in the construction documents cannot be expected of the contractor.

How detailed should the construction documents be?

The detail, form and length of the construction documents are a very important part of the contract with your builder. They should express in every aspect your intentions for the size and quality of the home you wish to build.

How specific should you be to communicate clearly? When the plans show a door to the bedroom, do they tell the contractor enough about the door to bid or build your home? You could tell him to use a wood door. Is it a flush door or is it paneled? Is it solid wood or a form of pressed board? The wood door could be described as a right-hand, long-leaf pine, interior-glued, doweled-joint, stile-and-rail construction, with four raised panels, undercut for return air venting, prehung on a pine frame with three brass hinges and c-11 interior head jamb trim pieces attached to one side, etc.

Think of the construction documents as a lease agreement when leasing an apartment. Some leases are a simple two-page document spelling out the broad responsibilities of the parties: who pays the rent and who maintains the plumbing. Other leases are a hundred pages or more in length, and every potential problem is discussed.

The detail, form and length of the construction documents should follow the same premise. They should be an appropriate expression of the owner's intentions. If you plan to build a mansion, and the plans and specifications are a couple of pages of roughly thrown-together drawings, not only will many of the details you wish to convey be left out, but also the builder will perceive you are trying to save money in every way you can. He can certainly save you money by leaving out things you thought were on the plans. Conversely, if you are trying to save money wherever possible and the builder and his subcontractors receive a forty-page set of plans, a two-inch-thick book of specifications and a long contract, you may cover yourself for potential problems, but the cost to construct your home will probably go up.

You and your designer must decide on the length, form and detail of the construction documents. Do you need a full, medium or builder's service? The more detailed the documents, the longer it takes to prepare them, and the higher the fee. Detailed documents are more thoroughly thought out and may avoid some confusion during construction—confusion that could cost much more than the documents themselves. Good planning will pay for itself over the course of the project. But of course I think that way: I am an architect and I get paid more for more planning. Discuss it with your designer and find a balance.

What are allowances?

When you have decided on a majority of your options for construction—such as room sizes and placement of doors and lights—but can't seem to make up your mind about the exact color or type of carpet, it is possible to make that decision after construction has commenced. But how will the carpet installer give you a good bid for his work without having this information? Carpet costs vary widely. What will he base his bid on? The answer is to provide an "allowance," a given amount of money, for you to spend later during construction. By allowing yourself enough money for the carpet material and installation, you can wait to select the carpet until it is time for the actual purchase, and still competitively bid your project.

If you provide an allowance of $5000 for kitchen appliances, you have this amount to buy those appliances. If perchance you spend $5500 for the appliances, overspending your allowance by $500, you will be required to come up with this

amount by some other means. You must either pay the difference in cash or find a savings of $500 somewhere else to offset
the amount (maybe underspending on another allowance). If you
have planned wisely and spent only $4000 on appliances, you
have $1000 either to spend on another item or to get a discount
off the total construction cost.

Allowances can be tricky and delicate. Project costs are
divided into two types: labor and materials. You should make
sure the allowance properly defines the work to be done. If
you've provided an allowance for carpet of $20 per square yard,
does the allowance include installation of the carpet or just the
carpet material itself?

It is best to quantify the allowance by specifying that the
amount is for material only (and the labor to install the material is
to be provided by the builder) or that the allowance is for both
labor and material. For example, if you wish to wait to make a
decision on the exact type of mantel for the fireplace, your
agreement with the builder could read: "Fireplace mantel allowance—$1900.00." After the builder spends $1800 for the mantel
(thinking the allowance was for material only) and $200 to install
it, you may find the allowance was overspent by $100. By simply
restating the allowance to read "Fireplace mantel allowance—
$1900 (labor and materials)," you avoid this discrepancy.

What standard is used to judge the quality of workmanship? How do you describe to someone the quality you want?

Most people will agree that a painting by Rembrandt is a
better-quality painting than a portrait of Elvis painted on black
velvet. But how could you describe the difference? You could not
say the Rembrandt is better because it is more expensive; a lot of

folks love Elvis and may pay a lot for the Elvis painting of their dreams. So how do you describe a Rembrandt without just showing it?

I know this is an exaggerated example of a quality standard. But if you are building a unique or expensive project, the quality of workmanship can be of great importance, and you must somehow communicate a standard for that quality. A written standard or exact sample is needed to judge the quality of work desired.

The written standard is normally a part of specifications prepared by the architect or builder and describes the quality of work to be performed. A written example of a quality standard can be as simple as, "The foundation slab must be flat." But how flat? Is there a better description than "flat"? Believe it or not, flat does not always mean what you think. A foundation slab covers a large area, and different areas of the slab can vary by fractions of an inch. It is impossible to make them exact. A fraction of an inch may not mean much to you, but to the framing subcontractor, and to the flooring subcontractor who must make the flooring level, a fraction of an inch and the addition of many fractions of an inch can make a big difference. A superior specification for flatness would be: "All corners of the foundation must be level within ⅛ of an inch of all corners and no area of the slab can vary more than ⅛ of an inch over an 8-foot span."

Other written standards of quality are those established by testing laboratories such as the ASTM (American Society of Testing Materials) or UL (Underwriters Laboratories). These testing labs have tested various materials and give standards of quality for wood, metal and concrete strengths and whether an electrical fixture is safe.

Another way of describing quality is by a photograph or an actual sample of the work to be done. If there exists a sample or picture whose "thousand words" can describe the quality you wish, it can be incorporated into the construction documents.

How one incorporates these into the documents should be discussed with the person creating them.

Since the specifications are part of the contract, a detailed set of specifications will greatly aid in clarifying quality.

Do I own the plans and specifications? I paid for them.

You may be surprised to find that although you pay an architect or home designer for his services, you do not actually own the plans and specifications he produces for you. In general, a designer's contract will show that the documents are owned by the person producing them, although you are provided with copies, even reproducible copies.

The original drawings of the plans are very important documents to both you and the architect. These are the standards by which all work will be judged in case of legal disputes. The architect will want to make sure no one inadvertently makes a change to the originals and reproduces the change over and over. If this is done, a great deal of confusion can be created about who actually made the change—you, the architect or the builder. Someone not qualified to draft or who does not know how to communicate in a graphic plan format may provide written misinformation.

CONSULTANTS
The Specialists

When do I need a structural engineer?

What keeps you from falling to the center of the earth? I know this is an easy question but of course it is the earth under your feet. But is quicksand considered earth? Quicksand is a special type of earth that doesn't support things very well. The earth of your construction site has its own unique characteristics, and every type of earth has been categorized for structural integrity by engineers over the years. It is important that your site be carefully considered by someone who knows the structural integrity of the ground it consists of. Will the earth on your site support the house you plan to build? Above the foundation, will the wooden first-floor walls support the second floor, the walls above it, the roof and the snow or person standing on it? If they will not, the foundation and structure may crack and fail.

This small lesson in structural engineering is to show you the importance of good structural design. The structural forces should be thought through carefully and the structure itself should be thoughtfully constructed. But a good structural design does not always require the expertise of a structural engineer. Just as you have the option to use an architect or a home designer, you have the option of relying on a structural engineer or the house framer. You and your chosen guide should decide which person will make structural design decisions. The more complex and critical the structural design, the greater the need for a professional. If your home will hang off the edge of a cliff or rest on unusual soil, I strongly recommend an engineer.

Whoever designs your foundation should be responsible for its structural integrity. If the foundation subcontractor designs and constructs your foundation, who would pay for its repair if it fails? Although there are other alternatives, I recommend a licensed, insured structural engineer for the design of any foundation.

I also recommend testing the soil of your site before designing a foundation. The expense of a soil test can far outweigh the expense of foundation repair and the possible resale stigma of a repaired foundation. A drilling truck will arrive at your site, take one or several core samples from the soil, take these samples to a laboratory and test them for various factors that will affect your foundation.

The structure above the foundation is equally important. There are several ways to design and construct the wood framing (wall studs, floor joints and roof rafters) and, depending on the foundation system required, an engineer may or may not be needed. Certain pier-and-beam foundations require that weights and loads be followed in precise detail, whereas some slab foundations can have more flexible configurations. Speak to your architect or builder about the pros and cons of using a structural engineer for work above the foundation.

What Is an MEP engineer and do I need one?

The MEP engineer is a mechanical (air conditioning/heating), electrical and plumbing engineer whose services are used in very few houses and are more often used in commercial construction. Someone, in any case, is responsible for designing the mechanical system, the electrical wiring layout and the plumbing layout and pipe sizes. There is a difference between subcontractors who perform the MEP work and those who do the foundation and framing. In most cities, anyone doing the highly specialized mechanical, electrical and plumbing work must be a certified mechanical contractor, electrician or plumbing contractor. These individuals have served as apprentices for various periods of time and were trained and certified to do their work. The foundation worker or framer is not always trained or certified in a similar manner.

In most homes, the mechanical system—the HVAC (heating, ventilating and air-conditioning system)—will be designed by the subcontractor who will install the system. Many mechanical subcontractors are employed by or have hired an engineer who will design the size of the equipment and the layout and size of ducts. Others will use standard design charts or base their designs on experience.

The electrical and plumbing work also will be designed by either an engineer or the subcontractors themselves. As with the mechanical system, the size and number of circuits, location and size of drains and water lines and where the vents will penetrate the roof will be determined by these individuals.

The architect will think through the mechanical system and give general information to the plumber and electrician for the design of their work. Your local building codes—minimum standards for your safety—also deal with these issues, since they affect the safety of the public.

What is an interior designer?

Someone, either during design or after construction begins, will need to select the exact color of your walls, the wallpaper patterns, the shape of the special dining room chandelier and the composition of the furniture layout. Many owners feel comfortable making these decisions on their own with the aid of their designer or builder. Others, however, wish to have the advice of someone with more experience or talent in these specific areas.

An interior designer (or interior decorator) is a specialist. He or she can order materials, furniture or fixtures directly from manufacturers or just give advice. Although the owner may wish to use the architect, few architects are familiar with the details of purchasing different types of wall covering or wish to be involved with these highly personal decisions.

When should an interior designer become involved?

The role you see the interior designer taking will determine when this consultant should be involved. If you wish the interior designer to have some input in the relationship of spaces and the size and layout of rooms and furniture, he should coordinate with the architect during the predesign and design process. It's better to have them involved during design than to try to remodel your new home during construction if the interior designer suggests major changes. Late design changes can be more costly during construction, since the coordination of work can be hindered.

If you desire the interior designer's aid only in selections of colors and finishes, he may not need to be involved until the last phases of construction. Even with the best designer's eye, selecting colors of rooms is difficult without actually walking through them. The full scale and shape of the room, as well as light coming through windows, can affect color and wallpaper selections.

How are engineers and interior designers paid?

In their classic roles, architects coordinate engineering consultants and pay them directly from their fee. For example, if the architect charges the owner a 10% fee for a full architectural service, the architect would hire those consultants to aid in the full-service design and pay them a portion of his 10% fee, ranging from 1% to 2%.

Another manner is for the consulting engineers to bill the architect for their services, and the architect in turn passes the cost directly to the owner as a reimbursable expense. Since engineers are not always used in residential work, and their services vary in scope from house to house, this reimbursable method has become more widely used.

Interior designers collect their money in several ways. They might bill for each hour of consulting advice, charge a fixed fee for their services or charge a mark-up fee for materials, fixtures or furniture you buy through them. Sometimes they charge a combination of the three. Ask them what their mark-up is for various items. In many instances they mark up items sold to you just as any retail outlet would, from 20 to 100% of the manufacturer's price. Although my feelings may be unfounded, I have always been a little suspicious of the interior designer who works only on a mark-up basis. They can pass from the role of designer/consultant to salesperson trying to make as many sales as possible, filling your home with items you don't want or need.

Where do I find good consultants?

Since most consultants work for you through your architect, home designer, builder or contractor, these people will be able to recommend plenty of consultants and when they should be brought into the design or construction phases of your project.

BIDDING AND NEGOTIATIONS

Selecting a Contractor and Arriving at the Contract Price

Should I go through the bidding process?

What if you were not planning on building a home, but were going to buy a new house already built? What if you were driving along a subdivision and spotted the house of your dreams just finished and for sale? You might almost have a wreck parking the car and running to inspect the house and site. Each room you go through is exactly what you want: the flow of the rooms, the feel of the spaces, the texture of the carpet. When you approach the sellers, you try to hide your excitement, because if they see how excited you are, they may not come off their offering price.

The sale of a new house is not unlike the sale of an automobile or a computer. The sale price is a mixture of the cost of the materials, the labor to put them together and the research and planning to design the product. But there is another large factor: the mark-up, or the cost of selling the product. Many computers whose total parts cost only $300 may sell for $2000. Some mark-up! Why would someone pay so much for something that costs so little? Because it's the computer he or she wants and no one will sell a similar one for any less. The logical end I am pointing to is the law of supply and demand. Manufacturers and distributors can charge so much because it's the American way. If enough people will pay $2000 for a computer, computers will sell for that much. If someone will pay $150 per square foot for a house, other houses of similar quality and location will cost the same. Conversely, if someone will pay only $50 per square foot for that $150-per-square-foot house and the seller can't wait any longer or is forced to sell, the house suddenly becomes worth $50 per square foot, even if the owner built the house for $100 per square foot. He will lose $50 for each square foot of house he is selling. This is the capitalist system at its best and worst—in this instance, best for the buyer and worst for the seller.

Back to your dream house. What makes it worth what the owner is selling it for? It's not just the cost to build it with a little profit on top. It's worth whatever you or someone else will pay for it.

Let's expand our example and make this dream house for sale by a builder. If he were wise, he would not build the house unless he could sell it for his building expenses plus some profit— a minimally reasonable profit to pay his bills and maintain or expand his lifestyle. What are the builder's expenses? The builder's expenses come from suppliers and subcontractors who are also doing work to make some reasonable profit to maintain or raise their lifestyles. The suppliers and subcontractors charge the builder the maximum amount they can without losing the work. The builder will sell the house to you the same way.

Suppose when you meet with the builder, you find that he is reputable and competent, so the house was probably built well. You also find that the house sells for $1,000,000—remember, it is a dream house. What if before waking up from this dream (or nightmare), you look out the window and see the exact same house directly next door? You rush next door, then tell the other builder the neighboring house is selling for $1,000,000 and you will buy either one. He smiles and offers his house for $980,000. What a deal—$20,000 off the other price!

After going back and forth watching the builders writhe and flinch, the prices settle at $550,000 for the first house and $540,000 for the second. You would finally go to the second builder and purchase the home feeling like the king of negotiations. In essence, the second builder either had lower costs in building the house or was willing to take less of a profit to sell it to you. The first either had higher expenses or decided to wait for the next person.

When you go through the bidding/negotiations process, all factors of the construction market, including supply and demand, go to work for you. Determining a price for your house is no different from the sale illustrated above. The contractors bidding your project will sharpen their pencils, cut costs and urge suppliers and subcontractors to do the same or they will not get the job.

What are some alternatives to the bidding/negotiations process?

Although the reader may perceive that I am in favor of the bidding/negotiations process, there are other ways of arriving at a cost of building your home without going through a formal bidding process.

One way is to select a contractor and arrive at a construction price with him only. Most contractors are reasonable and will be happy to explain fully their expenses and how they affect your project cost.

When you choose a contractor, just because you have selected the top person in the bidding-and-negotiations phase, it does not mean you have avoided the free-market system altogether. The contractor will still bid the remainder of the project among suppliers and subcontractors.

When you sign a fixed-fee contract with the builder, he is taking some risk that subcontractors could walk off the job or try to do the work for a higher price. The prudent builder will wait until construction commences before finally selecting the exact subs or suppliers to do the work. As time goes by, other suppliers and subs who may do the work for a lower price could come along, save money and possibly make the builder more profit. If you wish to receive the possible savings from work done later on the job, you must be willing to take some risk and have a "cost plus a fee" contract with the builder. Contracts in general are discussed in a later chapter.

In most situations the builder will use subs and suppliers with whom he has an ongoing working relationship, as long as their fees are not unusually high. The builder may know these subs are the only people in the area who can provide the quality of work demanded by you or him. However, most builders have a pool of subs and suppliers in constant competition for his work, and go for the best price.

If the contractor is selected up front, how do you know you are getting the best price? One way is to request he provide several bids between subs or suppliers to ensure he is looking out for your interests. You may even consider motivating the contractor to save you money by offering a bonus if he does. One such bonus could be that for each dollar he saves while maintaining quality, he earns part of the savings. By saving you money and *maintaining quality* he makes more money.

How many bidders should I get bids from?

The bidding and negotiations process can be time-consuming enough without having to deal with an enormous number of people. I recommend that a maximum of five people bid on your project. Three is manageable and will ensure you of good competition among contractors. Two contractors can diminish the amount of competition and may leave you with one bid. It is not unusual for one bidder to drop out late in the process.

What form should the bid take when I receive it? How can I tell if the bid is a good one?

You have waited two or more weeks since submitting your plans and specifications to several contractors. Some questions and clarifications about the plans and specifications probably arose from the contractors—mostly within the last week. When the specifications said to paint the entire house, did you mean paint the brick too? Your answer was yes, since you have always loved painted brick, but it was not clear on the specifications. Finally, all bids are brought to you in written form; you open them, and find all were under your budget. Great! Two builders are only $5000 apart, with the builder you like more being the higher one. However, the builder you felt uncertain about—the one who seemed a little unorganized—bid your house for $50,000 less than the others. How can he be so low? Did he make a mistake and leave the whole foundation cost out of the bid? If so, should you take advantage of it and sign the contract quickly, holding him to the mistake?

This is not an unusual situation for a homeowner. You should know more about the low bid before selecting the contractor. If he did make a mistake and you do sign a contract with him, after a few weeks of work he will discover his mistake and may threaten to leave the job. Unless you revise the contract, he could leave you with difficult delays and legal matters. When the bid you receive from each contractor is just a single maximum number, with no detail or breakdown of subs' and suppliers' costs, you can't know if there is a mistake or not.

Each bid should be broken down to include the various types of work, in order for you to compare the bids and, most important, to see if there are any mistakes. I recommend providing a bid form to each builder, similar to the example at the end of this book, and having each builder fill it out in detail to make the bid review process easier.

Some builders may find it inconvenient to use your bid form, since different builders keep track of their projects in different ways. Some bid the Sheetrock work together with the interior painting work. When they get a bid from a sub for all this work, it is lumped into one number. Other builders may bid this work separately. Because there is no standard way to keep track of bids, I also recommend that you preselect categories for the builders so you can tell at a glance that all parts of the project have been bid. This is also shown on the sample bid form.

If you had the three builders provide their bids on a bid form with preselected categories, you could tell at a glance that the builder who underbid by $50,000 did provide the foundation bid, that all areas of his bid were consistently 5% lower than the other bidders and that he also lowered his own fee, since he wanted to work for you so badly. You probably would feel better about his bid, and your reservations about his disorganization may diminish at the sight of saving money. Besides, you could find some other way to check his work and minimize your misgivings about his personality. You could, for instance, have your architect review the work in more detail to guard your interests.

What if the bid comes back over budget?

Nothing is more unnerving than sitting down, reviewing bids or estimates and finding all of them are too high. The last thing you want to think is "back to the drawing board." You can avoid this unfortunate problem during the design process by checking the budget several times, but in some cases the preliminary estimates for construction are off or something happens between the time the estimate is provided and the bids are taken. Sometimes a materials shortage or a change in the number of plumbers in the area will affect the bid, causing increase.

If your bids come in high, don't panic. The project is made up of hundreds of parts, and saving a little on most of those parts can do much. Sometimes, however, small portions of a project have a great deal of added cost, such as a special metal roofing or expensive flooring. Either way, costs can be cut more easily than most people think. The hard part is deciding which of your beloved features to give up.

In my experience, from 5 to 10% of the average project cost can be cut by playing what I call "the $500 game." The $500 game is one in which you find many items that can be changed in a minimal way and still not diminish the project or your quality standards. Lower the allowance for carpet: there are many carpet types and styles. Change the type or amount of wood trim around windows or doors. Delete the wainscoting in a certain room. Use Formica or another plastic laminate instead of the special kitchen counter. Select less expensive appliances. Wait to put in the special landscaping and go with minimal work, providing for future planting. All of these and many, many other tricks can save $500 or more. Again, if a large item can be done without, delete it from the cost of the project.

It can be very difficult to save more than 10% without some major revisions to the plans. The designer may need to redraw a portion of the house and decrease the size for the project to decrease a bid by more than 10%.

Can one competitively bid a project if the contract will be a cost-plus-a-fee type?

An alternative method of arriving at the construction cost of a project is to estimate construction costs and then use what is normally called a cost-plus-a-fee contract. In this case the contractor will give you an estimate of what he anticipates the job to cost, but will not guarantee this estimate as a maximum cost of the project. The only possible maximum cost in this scenario is the contractor's fee. He will build the project at his cost, plus a fee to coordinate the work. As long as subs or suppliers are not held to estimates, there can be no maximum fixed cost for the project, and bidding procedures are not necessary. If no one is held to his bid and rough estimates are taken, some contractors could be tempted to make unreasonably low estimates to entice you to use them and then share the bad news after you have started construction. More is discussed about cost-plus-a-fee procedures in the chapter called The Contract with the Contractor/Builder.

Doesn't bidding add a lot of extra time to the whole project?

When you decide to go through the bidding-and-negotiations phase of a project, you can anticipate adding a little time to the whole project, but the amount of time added, if any, is minimal. Other factors that determine the time spent on bidding are whether the contractor is preselected and whether he will in turn bid among his subs and suppliers or he will just pass the costs directly on to you and charge a fee.

As mentioned earlier, the only difference between bidding among builders and preselecting a builder who in turn bids among his subs and suppliers is that you are cutting out one stage of the bidding process. In my experience, a builder will bid a project by taking prices from his subs and suppliers, verifying them for accuracy, adding the price for special work he plans to do himself and then adding the normal fee for a project of this type. Depending on how much he wants your project—whether he is feeling the pinch of having no work or has too many jobs for him to coordinate—his fee will either be high or low for his standards.

Does the contractor have to pay for prints of construction documents he bids on?

Generally, printed copies of the plans, specifications and other information for bidding are given to the contractors free of charge, but they are responsible for keeping them from harm. You normally pay for the printing of all these documents and may need them back to give to the winning contractor. Care should be taken to keep them in good order.

During bidding, many people will require that the contractor provide a cash deposit to cover the cost of printing, an amount refunded after the documents are returned unharmed.

THE CONTRACT FOR CONSTRUCTION

The Agreement with your Contractor

What are the different kinds of agreements I can make with the contractor to build my home?

What if your project were under construction and you arrived at the site and noticed that the roof . . . looked a little strange. After you walked around the site you suddenly realized they put the wrong roof on your house. You distinctly remember telling the architect to tell the builder to tell the subcontractor that you changed your mind on the type of roof to put on.

Anticipating real problems such as these is the very reason contracts are written and signed. If there were no disputes, everyone communicated perfectly and everyone understood what he was to do and took responsibility for his actions, written contracts would not exist. But we unfortunately live in a fallen world; not everyone works ethically, and also honest mistakes are made. The contract for construction should lay out the various roles and responsibilities of the owner, architect, contractor and subcontractors and protect you from liability.

We have already mentioned that your agreement with the contractor includes the contract, drawn plans, written specifications and any other matter agreed upon by you and the contractor in written form. Several types of contracts exist, and the American Institute of Architects, your lawyer and your builder will have some for you to review, describing the responsibilities of each party and how the contractor should be paid. Unless you are familiar with written contracts, I suggest you speak to a lawyer or other qualified person before signing a contract with any party. A third-party adviser, paid by you, will look out for your interests only and can anticipate potential problems with the documents you are about to sign.

What is a fixed-price contract?

In a fixed-construction-cost contract, the contractor or builder guarantees that your project will cost no more and no less than a certain price. He has looked at your plans and specifications, received bids from subcontractors and suppliers, estimated a contingency fund and put all these costs together as a fixed price to build your house.

Your home is made up of thousands of pieces of material and hundreds of hours of labor. The prices of these commodities—labor and materials—are not always constant. They change daily over the months it takes to build your home. A wise builder will anticipate fluctuations in these prices and provide a pool of money, called a contingency fund, to cover a possible increase in costs of labor or materials. One of the major dividing factors between types of contracts involves who takes the risk for price variations and who receives the benefit of the contingency fund if it is not used up.

Since the contractor is guaranteeing the maximum price, he takes the risk that if prices increase during the course of the project, he may spend all of or more than the contingency fund. This risk entitles him to receive the benefit of the contingency fund if the price of labor and materials goes down over the same period of time. In essence, the contractor is taking some risk and hoping to make more money for himself. But you have the comfort of knowing you can afford the home. It will not cost more than the fixed construction cost unless you make changes that increase the cost.

What are the various types of cost-plus contracts?

COST PLUS

One way of taking the risk of rising construction costs away from the builder, thus taking it on yourself, is to use what is called a cost-plus contract. You pay for the individual costs of construct-ing your home, plus a fee to the contractor for coordinating the subcontractors and suppliers. This mark-up fee can be a percent-age of the total construction cost, such as 10% or 15%.

When the contractor receives bills from subs and suppliers, he passes them directly on to you, plus his percentage mark-up. If the prices of labor and materials increase during the project, your home will cost more. If they decrease, your home will cost less. You are thus taking the risk for the volatile cost of construction and in turn paying the extra price or saving the extra money. If you go in this direction, have your own contingency fund in case costs rise.

Many people feel uncomfortable with this unstable method of pricing a home, because there seems to be some motive for the contractor to get higher sub and supplier prices. The higher the labor and materials costs, the higher his fee: 15% of $200,000 is much more than 15% of $175,000.

COST PLUS WITH A FIXED FEE

One way to avoid having a builder raise the construction cost, and thus his fee, is to pay him a fixed cost for his services to coordinate the work. This will at least keep him from raising construction costs intentionally. If costs rise or fall, his fee will always be the same. Some folks, however, wish to motivate him to shop for better labor and materials costs, and thus to lower the overall cost of the home. Why should he do this favor for you? Obviously it plays well for him when you rave about him to other prospective clients, but there are more ways to motivate him to save you money.

One way to motivate the builder to look for bargains and lower labor and materials costs is to pay him to do it. Consider paying him an extra percentage of each dollar he saves you during construction. But beware: In the builder's, subcontractors' and suppliers' frenzy to save you money and make money for themselves, they may try to cut corners or leave out some work that was required by the construction documents, and the quality of your home may diminish. If you choose to go with a cost-plus contract and you are not familiar with interpreting plans and specifications, consider having your architect review the work as it progresses to ensure quality is being maintained.

COST PLUS WITH A MAXIMUM NOT TO EXCEED

The remaining variable, or risk, taken with a cost-plus contract is that the price of your home is not fixed. More important, there is no maximum, or cap, on how much your home will cost. You hope your builder has estimated the maximum cost conservatively, but if he has made a mistake, you may find your home increase in cost drastically in the middle of construction. Can you still afford it?

A less common extension of the cost-plus situation is to place a "maximum not to exceed" clause in the contract. By adding this clause to the contract, you are guaranteed that the cost of your home will not exceed a preset amount, and by using the cost-plus contract, you may have the opportunity to save money. You win both ways.

You can see that the contractor is beginning to take some risk again by fixing a maximum cost; however, many contractors feel so confident that their bids are correct and that the labor and materials market will remain unchanged, they will take this risk and sign this agreement. This may be the advantage he can offer over other contractors to get your job.

How is the quality of construction labor and materials spelled out in the contract?

Remember, the contract you have between yourself and the contractor is the written agreement, the plans describing the quantities of the materials and their locations and the specifications, which should describe the quality of the construction. Make sure your specifications address not only the types of materials (e.g., 2x4 wall studs) but also the handling, storage, installation and warranty of those materials. Not all specifications are this detailed. More is discussed about specifications in the chapter on construction documents.

FINANCING
The Money to Build It

Where can I find financing for my home?

There are more places to find financing for your home than you may think. Familiar places include the local savings and loan or bank. And even if you start your loans at these local levels, they may sell your loan to another institution somewhere across the nation. Selling loans to individuals or institutions is becoming more commonplace these days. By selling your loan, your bank passes the risk of financing on to the purchaser, freeing itself to make more loans.

In this time of growing private enterprise, a small class of personal mortgage bankers are arriving in the marketplace to act as your personal financing consultant, finding funds for your project. These people will find financing locally or nationally, and their fee is typically paid by the lender, not you. Lenders look for certain types of people for loans and are willing to pay a commission to find you. When an individual cannot find financing from the local savings and loans or banks, these mortgage bankers can do wonders. You may pay a little higher interest rate or a bigger down payment, but you will get a loan.

The Veterans Administration (VA) or other federal and local agencies often offer financing for individuals who meet certain qualifications. Most of these institutions provide special financing packages with low down payments or low interest rates, if you meet their criteria. Why not let your (or someone's else's) tax dollars go to work for you?

Credit unions, stock brokerage houses and wealthy friends or relatives are other places to go to finance your project, each offering different interest rates, terms and length of payoff. Research them all, find the best place for you and then negotiate on the interest rate or other terms. This is, after all, a relatively free market system. Let them compete for your business.

What does a financial institution need from me to approve financing?

If a stranger came to you to borrow a great deal of money, how would you make sure he'd pay you back? How would you retrieve that money if he could not pay? This is what concerns financial institutions when lending money. If they lend you money and you stop paying, what can they do to get their money back?

When you go to a bank to get a car loan, you go through a certain screening process. The bank wants to see that you can make the monthly payments. Asking how much money you make, how much you normally spend and what amount you have left after paying all your other debts will be a few such questions.

Once the bank is convinced you can pay back the car loan, it still wants to make sure it gets its money back if you, for some reason, can no longer pay. If you wish to purchase a car worth $10,000 on the open market, the bank may lend you only $8000 and ask you to give it a $2000 down payment. If for some reason it had to get the car back because of nonpayment, it would sell the car for as much as possible. When banks sell cars, they sell them quickly and do not always get the top price. Usually they will get only $8000 for your $10,000 car (and risk legal fees or other costs to have your car repossessed).

There is no real difference between financing a car and financing a house. The lender considers the same potential problems and how he will get his money back. If you borrow $150,000 for a home worth $200,000, their loan is fairly secure if they need to foreclose and sell your house. If you ask for $200,000 for a home worth $200,000, the lender may not be able to get enough money back. They must pay not only sales commission but high legal fees for foreclosure.

Lenders vary in the amount they will lend you for a mortgage; between 80 and 95% of the home's value is typical. If you apply for an $80,000 loan on a $100,000 house, the lender is lending 80% of the value of the house. Their risk is minimal.

What is an appraisal?

How does the lender know the value of a house before it is built? Only when a house is sold does one know its actual value. The value is the price a motivated seller will receive from a motivated buyer in a typical home sales transaction.

This is where a real estate appraiser comes in. This person researches and knows the housing market. The lending institution relies on this person's experienced opinion that the property could sell on the open market for a certain price. An appraiser will look at your plans and specifications, compare your house with similarly built homes that have recently sold in the area and come up with a value. Unless you can make a good case against this appraisal, this is the value the lending institution will use to make its loan. If your home appraises for $100,000 and the lender will lend you 80% of the value, you will receive a maximum loan of $80,000. You will have to come up with the difference as a down payment. If perchance your home appraises for $500,000, and your contractor can build it for $400,000, you may not need to come up with any down payment, since the lender's percentage criteria are met because of the appraisal.

Do I need two loans to build my home?

Believe it or not, most homes are built with two loans, not one. One is used to pay for the construction of the home, while the other pays off the first when construction is finished. Different banks and savings and loans make money in different ways, and some are regulated to restrict the kind of loans they can make. Typically the savings and loans make mortgage loans that you pay off over a long period of time. This lender is called the "permanent" lender; their loan lasts longest. Banks, on the other hand, are usually in the business to make short-term loans that must be paid back quickly. This lender is called the "interim" lender, since it lends money in the interim time between the start of the project and the completion of construction. When the home is finished and the short-term loan is due, the permanent lender (mortgage holder) will step in and pay off the interim lender (the bank). Your mortgage payments then begin. You do not make any mortgage payments until construction is completed and the interim lender is paid.

Suppose you wanted to build a home for $1,000,000 and could afford it (dream a little). After you design the home and know it could be built for $1,000,000, you go to a permanent lender (savings and loan or other) and apply for a mortgage. If you qualify and are approved, the lender will promise in writing to lends you the money for the finished home at a certain interest rate over a certain period of time. But it wants the home finished before giving out any money.

After the permanent lender commits to giving you a mortgage, you then would go to another source (typically a bank) for an interim loan to build the house. These lenders do not want to promise you a loan until they are assured they will be paid off by a permanent lender. They are in the short-term loan business, not long-term. When you show them your promise from the mortgage lender, sometimes called a "permanent take-out," they will promise to lend you the money for construction. At various stages during construction, the interim lender will release money to the builder to pay his subcontractors, his suppliers and himself.

After the project is completely built, the permanent lender is satisfied that the house is of the size and quality shown on the plans and specifications and no legal problems have been created during the construction process, the permanent lender will pay off the interim lender, and you will move in and start making mortgage payments.

This typical procedure is ever-changing, as the banking industry goes through continual reorganization. Many banks are now combining interim and permanent loans. In the future you may find one-stop shopping places for the money to build and mortgage your home.

How does the money flow during construction? Who writes the checks to whom?

A great deal of money changes hands from the beginning to the end of a project. For most people this is the largest single investment or outlay of money they will make during their lifetime. What I find incomprehensible is the casual manner with which many people treat the flow of money during construction. Many folks squabble more over the cost of an automobile than they do over the cash flow of their home.

Over the course of the project many people must be paid: the architect, contractor, subcontractors, laborers, material suppliers, bankers, lawyers, surveyors, printers, landowners, city officials, maybe even real estate brokers. These and other fees are part of the project's total budget financed by your home loan. The contractor pays those individuals whom he coordinates— usually his subcontractors, material suppliers, city officials for permits, possibly real estate brokers for referral commissions and designer. Other costs can be paid directly by the owner or through the contractor (to keep funds running through the construction budget, such as land costs, loan interest and lawyers fees or closing costs).

Before any checks are written from the construction bank account, certain procedures are normally followed. Below are some typical processes of cash changing hands for the various phases of the project.

A. Predesign, design and bidding/negotiations phases:
   1. The architect or designer bills you directly for services, and you pay him out of your own account. In most cases, financing to construct the house is pursued after plans are drawn.
   2. If arrangements are made to pay the architect or designer from bank financing, you can ask him to wait to be paid after financing is complete or pay him out of your own bank account before financing is secured. You can then reimburse yourself after financing.
   3. If the builder pays the designer, he will pay the design costs after signing a contract with you.

B. Construction phase:

1. After the work begins and the builder finishes a portion of construction work, he submits a "draw request" to draw (like water from a banking well) on your construction bank account.

2a. If the architect is involved as your representative, the builder submits the draw request to the architect before going to the bank. The architect goes to the site to review progress of the construction work, to see that the correct amount of money is being requested and to check whether the construction documents are being adhered to. The architect then recommends the amount of money to be given to the contractor and signs the draw request form. He then hands the approved form to the builder, owner or bank.

2b. If the architect is not involved, the bank may require you to sign the draw request yourself, showing you approve the amounts requested. You return the approved form to the bank.

3. If the bank you use has inspectors, it asks one of its inspectors to review the amount requested by the builder. If 50% of the construction has been done and the builder is asking for only 45% of the funds, the inspector will approve the draw request. If the builder is asking for 50% of the funds and only 40% of the project is complete, he will recommend funding only a portion of what the builder asks for.

4. With the signed approvals, the bank places the money into the construction account or the builder's account. The contractor can then write checks from either bank account to pay his people.

The whole draw request process can take five to ten days.

An important factor to note here is that although your general money flow is cared for by a bank inspector, the bank is not necessarily interested in whether the agreement between you and the contractor is followed strictly. It does not have the expertise to review construction, nor does it care to spend a great deal of time doing this. The bank is interested in the money flow only, not whether the kitchen sink is in the correct place.

CONSTRUCTION

Coordinating the Masses,
or The Fight of Your Life

How do I avoid the construction love triangle?

The love triangle is the mainstay of television soap operas. A lovely young lady needs one man to fulfill her intellectual needs but finds she also desires another handsome man. These two lucky fellows for some reason are also drawn to her. They vie for her affection, but unfortunately find that she will not choose one, she needs them both. Each man tries his best to convince her he is best for her and finds several ways to make the other man seem lower in her eyes. She has trouble keeping herself from playing favorites when it is to her advantage.

The construction phase of your project can become a soap opera if care is not taken. Even when you have no intention of creating a love triangle, you can find yourself in the middle very quickly. The residential architect and residential builder in general are independent types. Most have relatively small firms and enjoy a great deal of control over their projects. They take a great deal of pride in their work. Both feel they can be of service to you throughout the project and that they have your best interests at heart. If the construction communication process is not well organized, if the builder and architect are giving you conflicting advice and you don't know whom you should confide in, you have arrived in the construction soap opera zone.

The construction love triangle can be avoided by selecting a communication procedure before construction begins. There are several types of owner/architect/builder communications teams: owner/architect/builder; owner represented by architect/builder; builder/owner with architect as adviser in case of problems; and builder/owner with architect out of the picture.

OWNER/ARCHITECT/BUILDER TEAM

Pro: When the builder has worked closely with you and the architect from the beginning of the project, this relationship can work very well. At the beginning of some projects, you and your architect will meet together to create a design while including the builder in the process. The builder can act as a good resource when dealing with construction estimates at various stages of the design and also suggest easy methods of constructing details. When the builder is involved in the design, he also gets a good sense of your design priorities from the beginning, instead of trying to read them from working drawings.

When construction begins and the role of the builder is much greater, you and your architect can review the work as a team. When problems arise, all three can meet to discuss issues and reach solutions. Both the architect and the builder act as your travel guides, educating you about the process as it progresses.

Con: Potential problems exist with this team concept. If the builder takes a large role in design, he may step on the designer's toes. When the designer has a certain visual concept or idea and the builder is less trained in design and does not understand or care for the designer's concept, the builder may force his own ideas into the conversation and stifle creative interaction. Too many cooks can spoil the broth.

Similarly if the builder has much experience in the details of various construction procedures and finds the architect creating friction because he has an unproven method of construction to recommend, the architect can step over his bounds.

OWNER REPRESENTED BY ARCHITECT/BUILDER

When no builder is involved at the beginning of the project, or if the project will be competitively bid, you may choose to use this form of communication.

Pro: In the classic owner/architect relationship, the architect acts as your legal agent or representative from the beginning of predesign through the move-in. He acts as your personal travel guide and answers only to you. During construction, the builder and architect have a direct relationship, and you, although not left out of the communication process, deal mainly or only with the architect. A hierarchy of communication is created, with information flowing between you and the builder through the architect.

The owner who wishes to pursue this relationship either has little time to go through the long construction phases in detail or prefers to give the two professionals autonomy and merely be informed of progress. Problems are dealt with by the architect and builder. If a problem requires a decision on your part, it is the responsibility of the architect, your guide, to approach you.

In this procedure there is no likelihood of a triangle forming, as communication is linear, with the owner's representative in the middle. Of course, there is communication among all parties. When decisions or changes are made, the communication line is clear.

Con: This type of relationship between owner, architect and contractor has been developed over the past century, tried in the courts and found to be one of the best relationships. Your interests are guarded, and if the architect is fair, the contractor's interests can also be guarded. The only real problem with this process is that it costs the owner more money.

BUILDER/OWNER WITH ARCHITECT AS ADVISER IN CASE OF PROBLEMS

Pro: At the start of construction, the designer of the home has more knowledge of it than the contractor, and the contractor will ultimately have more knowledge of the construction somewhere in the middle of the project. The designer knows your intentions with the design and he knows his original intentions when drafting the plans and writing the specifications. The contractor, if just awarded the bid, is relatively new to the project. So having the designer visit the site and be available during construction can be very helpful to you and the contractor. He could find something the contractor missed or might anticipate a problem the contractor may have overlooked.

Con: This situation is almost linear when the builder and you deal directly with each other during construction and the architect is on call in case of problems. When a problem arises that you or the builder feels requires the architect, the architect is called to the site. The architect probably has not been included in solutions to other problems and may not have a good sense of how the construction has been progressing, or might possibly spot changes from the construction documents you were not aware of. Although his help is solicited, his viewpoint may be obscured by limited knowledge of the construction work or a sense of frustration that the plans have not been followed.

You can see that with this procedure, friction can lead to the tormented triangle. Even though you and the builder are closely linked, a few doubts created by the architect's observations (whether true or unfounded) can lead to minor distrust of the builder, leaving you in the middle of two desperately needed people.

BUILDER/OWNER WITH ARCHITECT
OUT OF THE PICTURE

Pro: If the owner goes to a builder first, and the builder in turn hires the designer or architect, the architect/designer is seldom involved during construction. The designer is a subcontractor to the builder, just like the plumber, and when he has produced the plans, thereby completing his services, he is no longer needed. He typically provides a builder's service and a minimal builder's set of construction documents.

The builder is in full charge from the beginning of design to the end of construction. When problems arise during construction, the construction documents are minimal enough to allow the builder to make the detail decisions. And since most problems with the construction work occur within the details, you, the owner, discuss the problems with the creator of the details, the builder.

Since only two people are involved during construction, there is no triangle.

Con: The worst problem created by this situation is when something goes wrong during construction and your are not familiar with the construction documents enough to interpret the plan and specifications. For example: A typical problem between a builder and designer is that the drawings are drawn a little differently from the way they were dimensioned. The dimensions are in feet and inches and show where the walls, windows and doors are. Sometimes a line is drawn a little to the left showing a wall ten feet from the edge of the house while the dimensions read that the wall is to be nine feet and six inches from the edge. When the contractor's framer looked at the discrepancy he assumed that the line is more important than the dimension, but this is not correct. Just as when you write a check and put the number to the side and spell out the amount below, the long-hand is the more important number. It is the policy of banks that when there is a discrepancy, the longhand number is respected. It is the same with plans. And how would you know to argue this point with a contractor without reading this book or having your architect to ask? I have found it interesting to watch an owner, who did not know how to read plans, and a builder, who also did not know how to read plans, argue over the misplacement of a stairway.

When major problems arise, and there are no checks and balances on the contractor's work and no one to guard your interests, whom do you turn to? Get help when you feel like the fox is guarding your hen house.

When construction starts, what happens first?

Whether your project is a small wood-framed home or a large multileveled estate, construction takes about the same course. You probably know that the foundation is built first and moving in is last, but few people know the steps in between. I'll try to give a brief description of the construction sequences, using some of the builder's terminology, so you can impress your architect and contractor.

Before any construction begins, before any worker sets foot on the site, before any materials are laid on the ground, the financing company will want to inspect the property to ensure that no work has begun. They want to be sure they have first-lien position, the first rights to the property if things go wrong. We will discuss liens (mechanic's and materialman's liens) in another question and your banker would be happy to explain their lien requirements further.

After the bank's "noncommencement inspection" the site is surveyed and the corners of the foundation are located. The survey is to ensure that the house is not accidently built over a property line, setback line or easement.

Once the foundation is "staked-out" (corners shown with stakes in the ground), the forming for the slab or the digging of the basement takes place. If the foundation is to be a concrete slab, the outside surfaces are formed with wood or metal. Next the first stage (rough-in) of the three stages of plumbing takes place. The water and waste water (sewer) pipes are brought to the exact place where the toilets and sinks are to be. Afterward the reinforcing steel bars (rebars) are placed in the forms, along with a vapor barrier to keep water from seeping through the concrete. The concrete is then poured.

The foundation concrete will usually sit for several days to allow it to cure, or harden. Concrete achieves most of its strength after a few days. Then the wood structural materials arrive on site and the "rough framing" begins. This is one of the most satisfying times of construction. It happens fairly quickly and the volume of spaces is first seen and felt. You can finally walk through the rooms. The framing work continues until the exterior walls are sheathed with insulation board or plywood, windows and exterior doors are "set" in place, the roof undersurface and the siding (if any) are applied and the exterior trim is installed. When the contractor reaches this point, the house is call "dried-in." The interior can remain fairly dry for the following work.

Near the end of rough framing, one of the three following phases of work begins. Either the "rough-in electrical" work, "top-out plumbing" or HVAC (heating, ventilation and air-conditioning) ductwork and equipment are installed. The plumbing topout work usually begins first. The water and waste-water lines are run through the rough framing, and the vents are run through the roof top (topped out). Sometime during the plumbing work, the roof work begins. The roofers can work fairly independently of the people on the inside and continue to weatherproof the house.

Sometime near the end of the plumbing topout, the HVAC installation crew will begin placing ductwork through the attic, basement (if you have one) and walls. The interior equipment (furnace) is sometimes placed along with the ducts. The exterior equipment is normally installed later—just before you move in— to keep it from "walking off" (being stolen) during construction. The first of the two stages of electrical work, rough-in, then takes place. The wall outlets, the light fixture boxes and all the wiring to be covered by the gyp-board (wallboard or Sheetrock) are installed. If there is masonry work to be applied to the framing, it normally begins near the end of the electrical work.

Once the guts have been installed the insulation work begins and covers much of the electrical and plumbing work. Afterward the "finishes" are installed. Sheetrock is "hung" on the walls and ceilings, the joints are taped and bedded (or floated) and a texture is either sprayed or rolled on. The cabinet work, interior doors and trim (all three termed the "millwork") are then installed and prepared for painting. Painting and staining then take place, followed by the installation of flooring. Following the flooring, the plumbing, HVAC and electrical "trim-out" begin. Plumbing fixtures are attached to the plumbing topout work, and the electrical lights, outlets and switches are installed. The HVAC grilles on the interior and the equipment at the exterior are set in place. The electrical and water meters are the last things to be installed.

There are dozens of further substeps left out that will affect the sequence of your particular house. For instance, the masonry fireplaces may be constructed before the roofing is applied to ensure that the flashing is done correctly, or the special stained and textured concrete flooring of your den may be poured at the beginning with the foundation and covered until the end to be sealed. Your contractor and architect can help you further.

How is a building permit issued?

Just before construction begins, the contractor takes the construction documents to the building inspection department at the city offices. These city officials review the plans for compliance with the various codes and ordinances and, if they pass, a building permit is issued. The price for this building permit is a tax that, in theory, is supposed to cover the cost of the building inspector's services and of bringing water and other utilities to your project.

What does the city building inspector do?

During construction a building inspector, a representative of the local city staff, is required to make sure certain portions of work conform to various codes and ordinances. For example, before any foundation work can be laid, the building inspector must confirm that the foundation is in the correct place and not overstepping any property or setback lines. It is only after the building inspector approves, in writing, that the inspection has been made that the contractor can proceed with the foundation. Similarly, after the insulation of the walls is complete, much later, the inspector must check the insulation before it can be covered with Sheetrock.

An important note about what the building inspector does not do. He is not looking to see that the plans and specifications are being strictly enforced. He is not looking out for your specific interests, but those of the city. His only responsibility is to make sure that the work meets minimal requirements of codes and zoning ordinances. The architect and builder are the only people who can help you here.

Who pays for various building permits?

Unless other arrangements are made, the builder normally pays for all permits, fees, licenses and other items pertaining to constructing your home. This is the usual term of a contract between an AIA contractor and an owner. But unless this is mentioned or written somewhere, the builder may not know it is his responsibility and may charge you extra for these items.

Who is in charge of the safety methods, techniques and safety precautions during construction?

In almost all cases, these responsibilities lie with the contractor or builder. Neither you nor the architect will be at the construction site enough to make sure all safety precautions are adhered to for the prevention of accidents. And though the designer may show how an aspect of construction will result, it is the contractor's job to choreograph the work. The plans, for instance, may indicate a 10-foot hole to be provided for a pier but not whether it will be dug with a shovel or a drilling rig. The drawings do not show how to guard against someone falling in the hole before it is filled either.

Who pays for problems or changes associated with concealed conditions?

Although you, the architect and the contractor may do everything possible to determine what work should be done to complete the project, sometimes something will show up that no one could have anticipated.

If, for example, on the first day of construction the contractor starts some excavation work and uncovers an old abandoned cave, should he be required to fill the cave so your foundation will be properly supported? Something must be done for the work to continue, but who should pay for it?

Even in cases where adequate research has been done, things like this occur. Since it would have taken a builder with a crystal ball to foretell this problem, much less estimate the cost to remedy it, he should not be required to pay for it.

What kinds of insurance should be purchased to cover construction work and who should pay for it?

The world of insurance is an ever-changing phenomenon, and a separate book could be written on this topic. My only recommendation is that you speak to a property and casualty insurance agent about various coverages and the risks you take during construction. The contractor should carry his own liability insurance, and some insurance related to your project, and should be required to pay for it out of his own pocket. You may also consider having your own coverage, just in case.

What are ways to avoid mismanagement or outright deception in money flow during construction?

The flow of money during construction can be easily mismanaged if not well organized and checked. It is your money flowing like water through a complicated piping system with clogs, backflow and, you hope no underground leaks siphoning off your funds. If you are not used to dealing with large sums of money or are not used to overseeing the construction process, I recommend creating a system of checks and balances to keep this important process under control. By releasing the money as the work progresses, instead of dumping all the money into the contractor's bank account at the outset, you add extra incentive for him and all his workers to do their work properly and stay on the job. If the builder leaves or goes broke, there should be enough money to finish the job.

Another way to avoid mismanagement is to have your representative review work done by the contractor before allocating any money to him. By having the architect review the work, you have hired someone who represents you, independent of the builder or bank, to make sure the project is being built as agreed. This is one of the only individuals who knows your project well enough to enforce the quality and quantity of work. The bank inspector is mainly concerned with quantity, not quality.

When a problem arises during construction, what should be done? Who best decides on the resolution?

What if you walked into your unfinished living room and found that the fireplace was built too far to the right and crowded the window to the point that your $1000 draperies would cover part of the fireplace? What should be done? Do you jump on the fireplace subcontractor and ask him to move it? Can the window be moved? Who pays to move the fireplace? Problems are unavoidable during construction. One or more of the two thousand decisions will be a wrong one—a sub could misread the plans or a critical piece of equipment could be misordered.

When something goes wrong, whom do you approach first? I suggest the following procedures:

1. Try to determine what the real problem is, without casting any blame or looking for who is at fault. Try to involve the architect and builder.
2. Consider various ways of solving the problem. Should the problem be removed and rebuilt correctly? Can the design be changed? Could the error be covered up aesthetically, or can the problem be ignored?
3. Discuss the costs associated with implementing the solution.
4. *After* going through procedures 1 through 3, try to determine who was at fault.

This process is a tried-and-true method. It is most times best to keep the project going instead of stopping work at every problem, causing a great deal of delays. Even though it is a normal reaction to search for who is at fault first and confront that person, a confrontation can cause a defensive response, a counterattack, possibly a full-blown argument and probably someone walking off the job. It would be much better to solve the problem and receive the advice of this knowledgeable person than to cause irrational actions, lose a worker, cause undue delay and probably add more cost to the project.

Good communication throughout the construction process is very important. When problems arise, all parties should be notified, and open honest discussion should take place to avoid an endless cycle of finger pointing. It is too easy to blame a person not present at the meeting.

Many times it is difficult to affix blame for a major construction problem when so many parties are involved. The completeness and depth of all the construction documents and the knowledge and competency of the person performing the task are just a few of the issues in determining who is at fault. In my experience, most problems occur when the drawings are not detailed enough to explain the work to be done, or the person doing the work cannot (or does not) read the drawings or specifications.

Hypothetically, when does a mistake in construction work become a problem? Not as soon as the mistake is made; it becomes a problem when someone notices the mistake. Until a problem is noticed, construction progresses merrily on its way, and what you don't know doesn't hurt you—until you get hurt. A good review process can help you spot overlooked mistakes and anticipate potential problems.

To determine what went wrong, one must know that the work is wrong, based on what was right. And the only way to know the right way to do the work is by going to the construction documents—the plans, specifications and contract—the only record of agreements for work required. If the work is not spelled out in the plans, the contractor cannot be required to build it. This is discussed more in the chapter called Construction Documents.

Why should I care if the builder pays his subcontractors?

When you sign your contract with the contractor, only two names are on the agreement: yours and the contractor's. None of the subcontractors or suppliers were present to sign, nor were they listed by name in the contract. The subcontractors and suppliers sign their own agreements with your contractor, and it is your contractor who is responsible for paying them, not you. When subcontractors do some work on the project, they each submit a bill to the contractor. The contractor combines those bills and presents them to you along with his own bill for coordinating the work, and you pay him. If after you pay the contractor he does not pay one of these subcontractors or suppliers, how could it affect you, since they have no direct contract with you?

One of the few resources a subcontractor or supplier has to get his money from an unscrupulous builder is to go to the courthouse and file a "mechanic's and materialman's lien" against *your* property. You have now become involved in the dispute between the contractor and this unpaid person.

What are mechanic's and materialman's liens and lien releases and how do they affect my project?

A lien is a claim against a piece of property. When someone files a lien against your property, he is claiming some of the rights you have to your property. You have suddenly lost a piece of your property, in that someone has legally claimed a piece of it.

The "mechanic's and materialman's" lien is the type of lien (or claim) a subcontractor or supplier is allowed to file against your property when he or she is not paid by your contractor. Filing a lien lets you know he was not paid and may create enough hassle for you to pressure your contractor to pay him. If he is not paid by the contractor after the lien is filed, the only way he may receive payment is either by filing a lawsuit against the contractor, or by claiming his portion of the money you receive at the sale of your house. If you are using a bank to finance construction of your home and the bank will be paid off by a mortgage company, this lien will be found before you go to your final mortgage closing. Many mortgage companies will not finance your home with a lien filed against it.

How can you make sure your contractor is paying his subcontractors and suppliers and guard against their filing liens against your property? The best way is to have your contractor provide you, your architect or the bank with something called a "lien release" each time money is paid to your contractor. A lien release is a document signed by the subcontractor or supplier promising the subs have been paid and will not file a lien on your property.

As construction progresses, this important documentation and paperwork can pile up. Keeping up with each payment to each subcontractor and supplier can get confusing. However, there is a shortcut; as with every shortcut, some risk is taken.

Your contractor can provide a written certification that he has paid all his subcontractors and suppliers. He thus promises that he is paying all the people on the job and that they will not file any liens on your property. The risk you take with this shortcut is that you may be taking the word of the person who is not paying his people. He may fill his coffers with their money and leave the job (and the state), while you find yourself with several unpaid subcontractors and suppliers and no money to pay them.

Most contractors are trustworthy. But if you do not know the person you are giving thousands of dollars to, check him out thoroughly and/or create a way to ensure that money is flowing where it should.

Do I need the architect or designer to review construction work, or is that the contractor's job?

Depending on the detail of the construction documents, the contract with the builder and your trust of the builder and architect, the architect can be of major or minor importance. As discussed earlier in this chapter, at the beginning of the construction work, the contractor has not had as much time as the designer to think of all that went into the plans. He may not be aware of your intentions and priorities. So during the bidding/

negotiations phase and the beginning of the construction phase, the architect knows the project much better than the contractor. There may be a time early or late during construction (again depending on the detail of the documents) when the contractor will know the project better than the designer. After all, he watches the construction every day, discussing problems with the subs, and knows every area in minute detail.

If the construction documents are a minimal builder's set and not very detailed, little is communicated to the builder. The builder will be making a great deal of the construction decisions. The designer may not need to be involved during construction. The builder in this case is dealing directly with the owner, and the designer is more or less out of the picture. The more detailed a set of construction documents, the more important the architect's role.

A different reason for additional construction review is that at various stages of construction the owner, architect, contractor and subcontractors suffer from different symptoms of not seeing the forest for the trees—or not seeing the trees for the forest. Depending on their point of view, they may not notice what someone else sees clearly. Someone not familiar with the construction process and procedures (usually the owner) can get a little lost in the rough construction stages, foundation reinforcing, rough framing and rough-in electrical. However, when it is time for wallpaper and floor applications, the owner can see the details much more clearly. The contractor during the first stages of construction can get caught up in the details of organizing the subs and may have trouble seeing big-picture items such as delays in the total construction time and how minor changes will affect work a few months ahead. On the other hand, the contractor, with the pressure of move-in time or a tight budget, can have trouble attending to the details at the end of construction. The architect, though definitely not the all-seeing and knowledgeable consultant, can add a good balance to the process, acting as the owner's representative and educated eyes to oversee the work, and as the contractor's mediator for quality standards if the owner expects too much or asks for a certain quality not agreed upon by the contractor and not specified in the construction documents.

What is retainage?

Have you ever hired a worker to do a minor job around the house and had him start the work, get to the middle and then leave and not come back for days? It happens too often. When an absentminded or unethical worker finds he can make more money elsewhere or work for less hassle, he will do it, leaving one poor soul stranded, demanding his return. If this worker was paid his entire fee up front, he is not as motivated to return and finish quickly. But if he has worked more than he has been paid for thus far, he may be motivated to finish his job or risk not receiving the remainder of his money.

Probably from the beginning of construction history, the builder and others relating to the construction profession have found that the "Golden Cruel Rule" is the best motivator to finish work: "He who has the gold makes the rule." Although many workers are very reliable, the few who cannot be trusted create problems. The only way to get them back to finish a job that may be holding up other workers is the knowledge that they may not get a good portion of their wages until they do.

One systematic means of motivation for the contractor, subs and suppliers is called retainage. You are detaining and retaining part of the money until they finish their work.

Another reason for holding back retainage is that during the time it takes to complete a project, certain subs rely on the work of other subs to do their work properly. For example, if the air-conditioning installer places an air vent on the ceiling in a way that it interferes with the special ceiling trim, someone has to move the vent. Since the work has to be done quickly to avoid undue delays, the contractor may ask the trim installer to move it. The trim installer will probably charge for his time to fix the air-conditioning man's mistake. If retainage has been withheld, the builder can deduct this added charge from what is retained from the air-conditioning man. The air-conditioning man may not complain about the small deduction, because it would have cost him more to travel to the job and change the work than to pay someone already there.

In many states laws require that retainage be withheld for all construction work to guard against an untrustworthy group. However, many people do not elect to withhold retainage because of undue hardship on the contractors and a possible monetary savings for themselves. Some subcontractors charge more if retainage is withheld.

The normal amount withheld for retainage is 10% of the work completed. If the contractor requests $30,000 for work verifiably done, then you or the bank will withhold $3000 until you have moved in. You can see the motive behind this law and the hardship created for a builder, especially if a project is relatively large. If the contractor's overhead and profit on a job are at 10% or slightly over that amount, and he may have to pay his subcontractors their full amount to keep them from walking off the job, his whole fee can be held hostage for the duration of the project.

Can I select or recommend my own subcontractors or suppliers?

Depending on the builder selected, you may have the option of recommending a subcontractor or supplier you know personally or who has been recommended to you. Most builders are in the market for people who do good work and welcome suggestions. However, you should give the contractor room to reject your recommendation. After all, he is the person with the power to hire and fire, and the subcontractor should work for him and not answer directly to you. The builder should not feel excessive pressure to hire someone close to you, since your friend may not be as experienced as his normal subs and may not be as reliable.

During construction, should I give instructions to the subcontractors or should I deal only with the builder or architect?

It is very important to follow strict lines of communication during the construction process. So many items are being dealt with and decisions being made that miscommunication can put a large wrench in the works.

The means of communication should be discussed in detail before any work begins and should be strictly followed until completion of the project. Even if it seems easier to tell the trim subcontractor to move a piece of wood trim without going through the channels, you may find later that he charged the general contractor for the trouble and that the builder has pre-sented you with a change order, placing his profit on top.

Depending on the arrangement you have with the architect or builder, you should deal with only one of them or make sure that both are kept informed of decisions. In the classic owner/architect relationship mentioned previously, the contract states that all correspondence to the contractor should pass through the architect. This can be a little extreme, but what may seem a small detail to you and the builder at the beginning stages of the work may cause great delays in the project later. At the beginning of the project, the builder is not as familiar with the work as is the designer, and even your well-intended suggestion may not be perceived as a problem. Moving a wall to the right just a few inches could change structural loads and cause them not to hit the foundation correctly. If the designer is out of the picture or is delegated to a minor role, you should deal directly and only with the general contractor.

Although being cordial and asking subcontractors questions is normal, harmless and even recommended for morale, if a subcontractor approaches you with a request for a decision, you should always have the contractor or architect present.

How long will it take to build my project?

The time to construct your project—as with the time to design it—depends on several factors: size, difficulty of the construction site, organization of the contractor's personnel, detail of the construction documents, number of projects the builder is involved with and the difficulty in reserving the artist to paint the mural of your great aunt on the ceiling, surrounded by angels. Though many factors need to be considered, some good estimates can be made if the project is well defined.

In general, smaller projects (1000 to 2000 square feet with minimal detail) can take three to five months from the time the lot is cleared to the time you move in. Larger projects (2000 square feet and up with more detail) can take four to ten months or more.

What if the contractor exceeds the time to build the project? Should he be penalized?

I strongly recommend that the builder of your project give you a time schedule showing how long it will take to finish the project so you can plan when to move in. Most builders will provide you with this information. Many folks have money at stake when it comes to the project completion date. They must close on the sale of their houses, or move out of rentals, and there may be termination dates on financing or other penalties for delaying the move-in date.

I also recommend having a system for tracking progress of construction to ensure the final move-in date, and having a plan B just in case the project goes overtime. After a certain point in the middle of the job the contractor can speed up work only a certain amount, and you don't want workers hurried into doing substandard work on your project. A few days' or weeks' delay is better than a lot of headaches after you are in.

A good system for keeping track of work progress is to have the builder give you a time line showing the various stages of work and the real dates (days of the month) that these stages will be finished. (An example of a time schedule is given at the end of this book.) You or your architect should keep track of these dates weekly, or every time the contractor is paid. By keeping this time schedule as the work progresses, you and the builder will be able to tell whether the move-in date is reachable.

Most contractors will give themselves a good time contingency (or slowdown factor) when making a time line. But when a bid is awarded on the basis of a short construction time, the contractor may not have allowed for slowdowns or may have made a mistake in calculating a move-in date.

Since many owners are materially or financially at risk if the project goes overtime, they will enter a penalty clause into the contract to motivate the builder to do the work within the time limit. One example penalty clause could have the builder pay the owner's rent or other expenses incurred for a delay in moving from their rental house. Other reasonable amounts may motivate the builder to finish on time, but the key term is *reasonable*. Make sure all costs are covered, but do not seek to profit from delays.

Any penalty clause should be discussed in detail with the contractor before signing a contract. Consideration should be given to the inconvenience to the owner and inconvenience to the contractor, who may need to pay for extra project-related expenses or overtime for employees to finish the job. A reasonable amount should be decided upon by both parties.

When a penalty for being late is decided upon, the question always arises whether the contractor should be compensated extra or given a bonus for finishing before the designated finishing date. If he can give you ample reason of monetary savings to you by completing the project early, then work out a bonus clause. In my experience, however, I have seen many penalty clauses but no bonus clauses. Please write to me with the exception.

If something goes drastically wrong, or the builder fails to correct some defective work, can I legally stop construction?

Although it seldom happens, some contractors will not change work that was done incorrectly, or will do something to disturb the owner to the point that the owner wants to stop construction. Unless this is addressed in the contract with your contractor, you may find you have trouble stopping the contractor from working. He may continue working without your consent and legally be due money for work you disapprove.

Whenever this situation is brewing, it is always best to proceed slowly, in writing, with a great deal of forethought and legal counsel. Stopping work can cost you and the builder a great deal of money in delays, loss of subcontractors, legal fees and other hassles.

What are change orders?

Over the long course of construction several people have a chance to change their mind and most of them do about something. Sometimes a problem arises during construction where changes to the contract documents are required. A change order is a change in the work to be done during the construction phase. As mentioned earlier, the written explanations of what the contractor is to do are the construction documents (plans, specifications, contracts, etc.). So any change in the work is a change in the construction documents. If the garage was drawn to be 24 feet wide and, after the work has started, you decide it needs to be 30 feet wide, to make this change requires a change order. You are ordering the contractor to change the work in a certain manner. Of course enlarging the garage by six feet will cost more money and may cause the project to take longer to finish, so the final construction cost and completion date also must be adjusted and agreed upon.

Even if the change is minor, a written record of the change should be made to protect both you and the contractor. Any written record of a change can be a change order, but there are standard forms, which easily modify the construction contract. Since the time it takes to build a house is long and memories are short, it saves a lot of headaches and stress to have in hand a sheet of paper showing that a change would save $100 when you may remember distinctly hearing the contractor say the change would cost nothing.

In most cases when a change order is completed, the contractor's overhead, profit and a "hassle" factor are added to the change-order cost. The hassle factor is the additional time the contractor takes to speak to subcontractors and estimate the time and expense of implementing the change. All the additional expenses incurred for a change-order range from 10 to 20% of the actual change-order amount.

Sometimes a change order results in a decrease, not an increase, in the final construction cost. In these cases, even though the contractor must go through the same procedures to save you money and justifiably deserves some compensation, he will not charge you for this type of change order.

What is my role during construction?

The construction phase is a very exciting time for everyone involved. What was in everyone's imagination is now taking shape. You are actually walking through what you dreamed of just a few weeks before.

Depending on the role you have chosen for yourself, your designer and your builder, your participation may vary. This book mentions several roles of all the players in the construction process, and you may choose a combination of all of them. In each case your role is very important. You can help or hinder the construction process with your presence on the site.

Since it is *your* money being spent, you should take as big an interest in what is going on as anyone: the designer, builder, subcontractor, banker, and so forth. Make sure you stay in touch with your hired guides; keep your eyes open for potential problems; make sure it is looking like you imagined it; but most of all keep communication lines in an orderly manner and *stay within the communication processes* you decided upon before construction began.

Many an owner has created morale problems by arriving at the site, frowning and complaining to the subcontractors about their work. The wise owner will wait and express his concerns to the architect or builder, who will either explain what the subs are doing or correct the work through the proper channels.

When the owner goes to the construction site, it is an excellent time to motivate subcontractors and create good will.

Meet the workers without getting in their way, bring them a snack or drink, show your true excitement about how the project is going and how the subcontractors' role is making your dream come true. Subcontractors may work a little harder when they feel closer to the owner. If something goes wrong, they may not wish to let a friendly person down, but if you treat them indifferently or complain about their work, they may not care. They go home and leave your problems at work—your home.

Doing these simple things will make the project go much more smoothly for everyone, which is in your best interest.

What kind of records should I keep during construction?

I recommend keeping several types of records in different file folders during the design and construction process. Recording decisions, ideas and problems makes it easier to remember and refer to them a few months or a few years from now. Not all records need to be kept for years, even though some have advantages that far in the future.

Following are some recommended files:

1. Contracts
   Keep a copy of all agreements between you and any other party related to the project—the builder, the architect and any consultants.

2. Design
   During the design process many ideas are tossed about and many decisions are made. Keep a copy of all drawings and correspondence between you and the designer. This file may be bulky if design ideas are presented on large sheets of paper. If so, have them folded or rolled up together and marked for easy reference.

3. Construction Documents

   A copy of the original construction documents may also be on several types of paper. I recommend keeping the letter-size contract in the contracts file and the larger working drawings or blueprints nearby. The specifications are best rolled up with the drawings to keep them together, since they directly relate to each other.

4. Draw Requests and Timetable

   Each draw request from the builder should be numbered and filed, while the time schedule for construction should be updated with every draw request.

5. Construction Receipts

   When work is done with a cost-plus-a-fee contract, the receipts are extremely important. They are the record of the amounts you fund to the builder. But in other instances some builders will give you copies of their receipts from their subcontractors, just to inform you that the work was done for the budgeted price.

6. Photographs of Construction in Progress

   I recommend taking a camera with you as you go to the construction site. Take many pictures to create a catalogue of the work. The most important times to take photographs of the work are: before any work is started and the site is clear; directly before any foundation concrete is poured; just before the insulation is placed in the wood framing and you can see all the wiring, plumbing pipes, air-conditioning ducts, wood walls, floors, ceilings and roof; directly after the insulation is put in and before the sheetrock is applied; and at various times while the exterior and interior surfaces are being installed. These records will not only be useful if some problem is found with the work that is covered, but can be of great use in the future if you wish to remodel the house. The remodeling designer or builder may need to know exactly how a certain area of the house was put together.

7. Financing and Closing
Also keep good records of correspondence with the bank and other agents or consultants.

8. Warranties
Most of the mechanical equipment and appliances and some of the other materials you place in the house will have warranties. Keep these together for easy future reference.

9. Chronological List of Changes and Discussions
I highly recommend that when you meet with the architect or builder during construction a list be kept of issues discussed and changes mentioned, even the most minor changes. Each item should have its own number, the date when first discussed, possibly a date for each additional time it was mentioned and a description of the item. It is extremely difficult to remember minor yet important, things from two months ago while walking on the job site. An example of this is attached with the exhibits at the end of this book. This list can also become the final punch list at the end of the project.

What Is a punch list and who makes It?

Although you may make a list of everyone you want to punch at the end of the construction process, this is a different type of punch list. At the end of construction, just before you move in (or sometimes just after you move in), there will be several items for the builder to complete before the house is considered finished. There are always some areas where the painters need to touch up; there are some loose ends to finish, such as applying the cabinet pulls on the drawers. Sometimes there are larger tasks to be completed, such as replacing the dented gutter or moving an air-conditioning system that was installed in the wrong place.

The list of tasks to be performed is called a "punch list." As the builder finishes each item it is checked off as complete. It was probably originally called a punch list because the list of items was punched like a punch card as each item was finished.

When there are several people reviewing the work, there are probably several lists being created. The builder has his list, the owners have theirs and the architect has another. All these lists should be discussed with the builder, agreed upon and combined into one final punch list. When the builder finishes these tasks, the work is considered complete. Since the work is complete, the final payment could be made to the builder.

Anything found needing attention after the final payment is made is considered warranty work and treated in a different manner.

MOVE-IN AND BEYOND

Staking Your Domain

Should I do anything other than just inhabit the house?

After the final punch-list item has been tended to and you move into the house, you will probably notice more details that are unfinished, ones that missed the eye of the contractor and architect. And you will continue to see these for the first few months you live in the house. What you should do is create another list of warranty items for the contractor, subcontractors or suppliers.

As you occupy the house problems will reveal themselves. The thermostat may stop working, a light fixture may overheat, you may notice a leaky area at the exterior trim. List all these items.

I recommend waiting for a month or so before asking the contractor to repair the work. This will be much easier for everyone. Instead of coordinating subcontractors and suppliers each week as new problems arise, the work will be done in a more organized manner and your home life will be less disrupted.

Even though you may wait before having the workmen do their work, I recommend updating the contractor on the list on a weekly basis. As you notice work to be done, there may be something that seems insignificant to you but may cause a lot of damage if not repaired immediately. Only the contractor or architect can tell which issues are especially important. And keeping the contractor aware of the problems on a weekly basis can avoid some disasters. Although most of the work will be done a month from now, the important work will be done quickly.

What warranties are there for my home?

Warranties occupy a great percentage of any automobile commercial, and each manufacturer offers a variety of warranties to attract the buyer. There are 50,000-mile warranties on the engines, 12,000-mile warranties on some parts and lifetime warranties on others. It can get confusing. But what about a home warranty on the construction of a house? The equipment usually has a warranty. The HVAC system, electrical equipment, roofing and appliances have written warranties, but what about the aluminum siding, paint, wallpaper or flashing? Who pays for repairing these items when they have been installed incorrectly?

Unless it is written in the contract, there is no real warranty for the contractor's work. You may be lucky to have a builder who will follow through on warranty work with no warranty but if something went extremely wrong, there is no legal document to fall back on. Most AIA contracts require a one-year warranty on all work performed by the contractor.

What if your contractor goes broke in the middle of your warranty period? In these financially unstable times it happens quite a bit. You may wish to have more protection than a contract with the builder. Although this problem makes a good case for hiring a contractor with a long history of satisfied customers, even those contractors stumble.

There are several programs available from national organizations that provide this service. The Home Owner's Warranty (H.O.W.) is an example of this extended warranty. I recommend speaking to your builder or the National Association of Home Builders (NAHB) about these options.

How do I follow through on warranty claims?

When you move into your house, your builder should give you a list of your major subcontractors and suppliers—the electrician, HVAC contractor, plumber, cabinet fabricator, roofer, brick mason, landscape installer, foundation contractor, framer, appliance supplier, and so on. After the contractor's warranty expires, there will be equipment and other warranties that remain in effect. If a problem arises call the supplier or subcontractor who did the work. He will help you with maintenance or warranties associated with their work.

REPRESENTATION
The Best Guide for Your Situation

Whom should I go to first—the architect or the builder?

If you have read this far through the book and not just jumped to the ending, you probably have a good idea of whom you should go to first. The question is a complicated one that requires a good knowledge of the design and construction process.

Everybody has an opinion on this topic. Some have had bad experiences or know of friends who had trouble with a "prima donna" architect who designed a monument to his ego and dismissed the owner's requests as "in the way of his vision for the project." Others have had experiences with a builder who was seldom at the project site and allowed less experienced subs to go unchecked or tried to get extra money at the end of the project because of unsubstantiated change orders. Some know either architects or builders personally or socially and make judgments based on nonconstruction factors.

No matter what you hear, whom you should go to first is a complicated question. The type of project and how you wish to be advised in the many phases of the process will determine the answer. Many issues must be discussed before taking this first step. Some small, less expensive projects typically begin with a builder—but not necessarily because the project is small. Some of the smallest projects need the expertise of a designer, trained for the job. Many large, more expensive projects start with an architect and eventually get bid upon by several contractors, but even some of the largest projects can be built with minimal use of an architect or designer.

How open should I be with the builder or architect about what I can afford?

If you were in the market for a new car and knew that car prices were negotiable, would you go to the only dealer in town and tell him, "All the money I have is $20,000. What can I buy?" You bet he could find you a car for $20,000, even if it normally sold for $18,000. In a similar vein, you could approach a builder and tell him, "I only have so much money to spend. Would you build the most house you can?" "Sure," he could say grinning from ear to ear, "I'll do my best."

I apologize to honest builders everywhere for comparing them to car salesmen (I don't necessarily apologize to the car salesmen). Many builders will try their best to get you the best home for your money, but a few get a little greedy and find you an easy target to maximize their profits. If they know there is no other competition for your work, for instance, they can pretty much charge you what they wish. Similarly, if your plans and specifications were in order and you asked one builder to get a bid together for your home, would you tell him your maximum budget was $100,000 before he bid it? What if he were about to bid your project at $75,000 before you told him? His pencil probably wouldn't get real sharp when he put those final figures together. If you then went shopping for another builder and told him the same thing, not mentioning any competition, he might be a little more honest with his figures, but unless he is a builder of high integrity, his bid may come real close to your maximum budget.

There are two points I am trying to make with this argument: One is that a loose, shopping-like bidding process will not get you the best value for your home. Secondly, in a noncompetitive situation, you may not want to play all your cards at the beginning of the game.

What about the designer or architect you select to design your home? Should you tell him your maximum budget? If the designer works directly for the builder who will eventually build your home, you should probably speak cautiously to him. If, however, you plan on competitively bidding your home among several builders, you should feel free to share this information with them. As long as they hold it in confidence and do not share it with the prospective bidders, you are protected.

How do the contractor and architect work together?

In many cases the architect and contractor can work well together from the beginning to the end of a project. If discussion and definition of each other's roles (who is in control of image and/or who is the recommender of alternative construction solutions) are dealt with at the first meeting of the project, a good possibility exists that the two can work well together throughout.

Eventually the architect and contractor will work together on the project. The question should really be, "How can the architect and contractor work best together?'' and the answer again is: It depends. There are many ways the contractor and architect can work well together.

During the construction phase, roles should be clearly defined by the contract. In the classical full-service role, the contractor will coordinate construction of the project, and the architect will act as your legal agent to observe the work, approve or disapprove amounts of money the contractor is paid, and keep the owner apprised of the quality and progress of the work. When conflicts arise, the architect acts as your representative to educate you about the problem and act as arbiter when conflicts reach an impasse.

When the project is complete, you, the architect and the contractor go through a punch list (or detailed list of items to be finished) before the project is considered complete. It is then your responsibility to deal with the financial institution for transfer of permanent funds and finally move in.

Why so much dissension between architects and builders?

Many people have heard that architects and builders do not enjoy working with each other but are forced into a marriage of convenience by the owner, who needs them both. But this is not always the case, and this question may overstate the problem. Even so, in some cases hostility and outright hatred exist between the two professionals.

I feel that most of the ill will between architects and builders is a lack of communication and appreciation and understanding of each other's role. Other factors can contribute to the problems, such as the differences in training and experience of the builder and architect and personality conflicts.

When a project is started without open, honest and thorough communication, there is a very good chance that the project will be a great hassle for all involved: the architect, who designed it and wants to make sure his conception is brought to fruition; the builder, who takes great pride in fabricating a building with efficiency and style; and the owner, who feels that the whole process is out of control and prays it will end without two dead professionals and a structurally unstable home.

Many builders can remember trying to build something designed by an inexperienced designer or an intern architect, fresh out of school, who thinks he knows more than he really does about the construction process. Most architectural schools train their students in design, structural and legal issues related to architecture and leave the further education of their young interns to their apprenticeships. The details of construction methods are always changing, and for the required years of internship before an intern can become a registered architect, the intern is learning the particulars of how buildings actually go together. A young, inexperienced architect can be a dangerous person if he acts beyond his experience or is unsupervised.

Many architects, on the other hand, recall trying to explain one of their tried-and-true details to an inexperienced contractor. Some builders resent or suspect other construction methods forced upon them by someone they may not know, even if other builders have used them for years.

Builders and architects probably were attracted to their professions because of their distinct personalities. In my experience, many (but definitely not all) builders are very practical by nature and enjoy the nuts and bolts of how thing go together. In modern terms they would be called left-brain-dominant, linear thinkers and type A personalities. Architects, on the other hand (but, again, not all architects), are more intuitive or creative by nature and enjoy the dreaming and conception of the spaces they will soon walk through. In modern terms, they would be called right-brain-dominant, intuitive thinkers and type B personalities.

In the building profession, unlike life, opposites do not always attract. Not all professionals are looking for that perfect complement to their personality to make their life complete. And as long as these two personalities do not meet with openness and honesty, dissension will continue.

Closing Remarks

I know we have covered a lot of ground since the introduction, so please continue to refer to this book at the various stages of design and construction. The whole process takes several months, memories are short and misunderstandings come too easily without a good knowledge of the process and good communication between you, the architect and the contractor. My hope is that the information shared in this book was a good first step that will lead to a successfully constructed project and the home of your dreams.

EXHIBITS

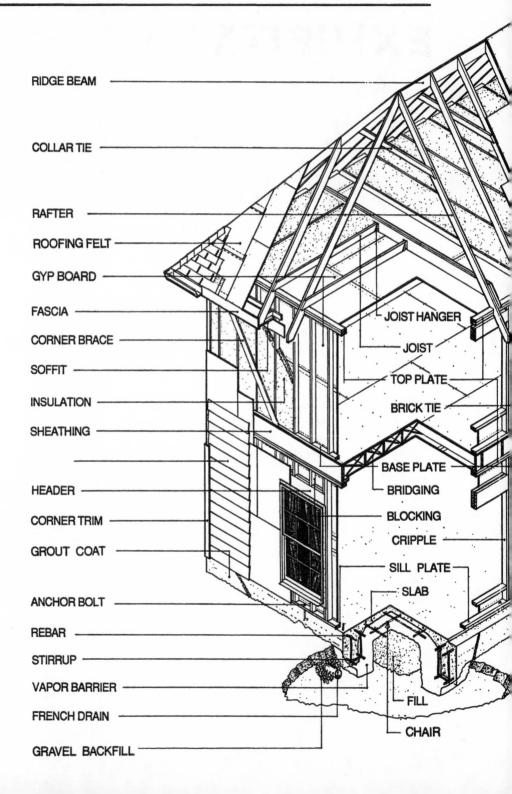

RIDGE BEAM

COLLAR TIE

RAFTER

ROOFING FELT

GYP BOARD

FASCIA

CORNER BRACE

SOFFIT

INSULATION

SHEATHING

HEADER

CORNER TRIM

GROUT COAT

ANCHOR BOLT

REBAR

STIRRUP

VAPOR BARRIER

FRENCH DRAIN

GRAVEL BACKFILL

JOIST HANGER

JOIST

TOP PLATE

BRICK TIE

BASE PLATE

BRIDGING

BLOCKING

CRIPPLE

SILL PLATE

SLAB

FILL

CHAIR

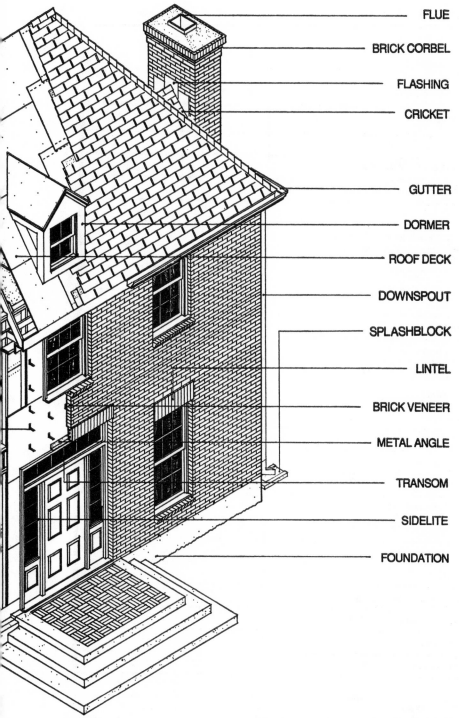

FLUE

BRICK CORBEL

FLASHING

CRICKET

GUTTER

DORMER

ROOF DECK

DOWNSPOUT

SPLASHBLOCK

LINTEL

BRICK VENEER

METAL ANGLE

TRANSOM

SIDELITE

FOUNDATION

BID FORM

ITEM NO.	DESCRIPTION	VOLUME	PRICE
1	Site Work		
2	Surveys and Excavation		
3	Flatwork, Ret. Walls and Curbs		
4	Permits, Taps and Other Fees		
5	Foundation		
6	Framing Material and Trusses		
7	Framing Labor		
8	Masonry		
9	Roofing		
10	Windows		
11	Doors Interior and Exterior		
12	Garage Doors		
13	Insulation		
14	Metal Work		
15	Drywall, Tape and Float		
16	Painting		
17	Plumbing Labor and Materials		
18	Plumbing Fixtures		
19	Electrical Labor and Materials		
20	Electrical Fixtures		
21	HVAC		
22	Cabinets and Counter tops		
23	Trim Material and Shutters		
24	Trim Labor		
25	Ceramic Tile		
26	Vinyl Flooring		
27	Wood Flooring		

Signed   Title   Date

BID FORM

ITEM NO.	DESCRIPTION	VOLUME	PRICE
1	Site Work		$ 2596
2	Surveys and Excavation		3,678
3	Flatwork, Ret. Walls and Curbs		1,221
4	Permits, Taps and Other Fees		459
5	Foundation	3000 sf	15,908
6	Framing Material and Trusses		24,989
7	Framing Labor		20,000
8	Masonry		10,983
9	Roofing	40 square	4,928
10	Windows		12,900
11	Doors Interior and Exterior		15,908
12	Garage Doors		1,100
13	Insulation		2,900
14	Metal Work		1,000
15	Drywall, Tape and Float		6,999
16	Painting		13,865
17	Plumbing Labor and Materials		12,000
18	Plumbing Fixtures		5,000
19	Electrical Labor and Materials		7,040
20	Electrical Fixtures	allowance	3,500
21	HVAC	4 tons	9,975
22	Cabinets and Counter tops		10,000
23	Trim Material and Shutters		4,876
24	Trim Labor		5,111
25	Ceramic Tile		800
26	Vinyl Flooring	200 sf	400
27	Wood Flooring	800 sf	4,800

Signed   Title   Date

BID FORM

ITEM NO.	DESCRIPTION	VOLUME	PRICE
28	Tile Flooring		
29	Carpet		
30	Mirrors and Glass		
31	Clean Up		
32	Other (specify)		
33	Other (specify)		
34	Other (specify)		
35	Other (specify)		
36	Other (specify)		
37	Other (specify)		
38			
39			
40			
41			
42	All Lump Sum Allowances - total		
43			
44			
45			
46	Contingency - If Any		
47	Supervision - If Any		
48	Contractor's Overhead and Profit	(_____%)	
49	Insurance		
50			

Total Lump Sum Base Bid

Dollars
_____

$ _____

_____

Signed   Title   Date

BID FORM

ITEM NO.	DESCRIPTION	VOLUME	PRICE
28	Tile Flooring		600
29	Carpet	200 sq yds	4,000
30	Mirrors and Glass		1,900
31	Clean Up		576
32	Other (specify) Special Hardware		800
33	Other (specify) Pool allowance		30,000
34	Other (specify) Copper gutters	1000 lin ft	10,200
35	Other (specify)		
36	Other (specify)		
37	Other (specify)		
38			
39			
40			
41			
42	All Lump Sum Allowances - total		10,000
43			
44			
45			
46	Contingency - If Any		5,000
47	Supervision - If Any		6,000
48	Contractor's Overhead and Profit	(10 %)	23,472
49	Insurance		
50			

Total Lump Sum Base Bid

Two hundred sixty nine thousand, two hundred twenty two   Dollars

$ 269,224

Signed   Title   Date

PROJECT SCHEDULE

Project: _____

Page: _____

Month

Activity
Start with earliest

proposed
actual

1st to 7th	8th to 15th	16th to 23rd	24th to End

(table columns repeated for seven months: 1st to 7th, 8th to 15th, 16th to 23rd, 24th to End)

PROJECT SCHEDULE

Project: Smith Residence   Page: 1 of 1

Month	May						June						July						August						September						October			
Activity Start with earliest	1st to 7th	8th to 15th	16th to 23rd	24th to End			1st to 7th	8th to 15th	16th to 23rd	24th to End			1st to 7th	8th to 15th	16th to 23rd	24th to End			1st to 7th	8th to 15th	16th to 23rd	24th to End			1st to 7th	8th to 15th	16th to 23rd	24th to End			1st to 7th	8th to 15th	16th to 23rd	24th to End
Site Prep																																		
Foundation																																		
Framing																																		
Plumbing																																		
HVAC																																		
Electrical																																		
Roofing																																		
Siding																																		
Masonry																																		
Sheetrock																																		
Exterior Paint																																		
Interior Trim																																		
Cabinetry																																		
Interior Paint																																		
Floor finishes																																		
Touch up painting																																		
Final clean up																																		

(each activity row shows "proposed" and "actual" bars)

GLOSSARY OF BUILDING TERMS

Below are listed a few of the more frequently used terms of construction. This is by no means a complete list.

acoustical ceiling spray. The textured mixture sprayed on the ceiling as the finish that helps reduce sound transmission.

AIA. Abbreviation for the American Institute of Architects.

anchor bolt. A threaded fastener embedded in the concrete used to secure another part of the building to it.

apron. A paved area, such as the juncture of a driveway with the street or with a garage entrance.

backfill. Gravel or soil that is placed in an area previously excavated.

baseplate. A horizontal wood member that serves as the bottom tie in a stud wall partition.

batter board. One of a pair of horizontal boards that are nailed (at right angles to each other) to three posts set beyond the corners of the building excavation. They are set up at the corners of the building and connected by strings. The intersections of the strings indicate the precise location of the building corners.

beam. One of the principal horizontal wood or steel members of the structural system.

bearing wall. A wall that supports an imposed load such as a floor or a roof of a building.

blocking. Pieces of wood to secure, join or reinforce members or to fill spaces.

brick tie. A metal strap used to secure the brick veneer to the structural component of the building.

brick veneer. Brick that is used as the outer surface of a framed wall and is nonstructural.

bridging. A brace or system of braces placed between joists to stiffen them, to hold them in place and to help distribute the load.

building paper. Heavy paper used in walls or roofs to damp-proof.

built-up beam, timber. A timber made up of several pieces fastened together, forming one of larger dimensions. See also glue-laminated beam.

chair. A metal or plastic piece used to raise the reinforcing steel off the ground.

collar tie. A horizontal member that ties together (and stiffens) two opposite common rafters, usually at a point near the top of the rafter.

column. In structures, a relatively long, slender structural compression member such as a post, a pillar or a strut; usually vertical, supporting a load, it acts in the direction of its longitudinal axis.

condenser, condensing unit. The portion of the HVAC unit outside the building, which cools the refrigerant for the air-conditioning.

corner brace. A diagonal brace let into the studs to reinforce the corners of a wood-frame house.

cornice. The exterior trim of a structure at the meeting of the roof and wall; usually consists of bed molding, soffit, fascia and crown molding.

cricket. A small saddle-shaped projection on a sloping roof used to divert water around an obstacle such as a chimney.

cripple. In a building frame, a structural element that is shorter than usual, as a stud above a door opening or below a windowsill.

deadwood. Pieces of wood nailed to the frame to which the Sheetrock is attached.

escutcheon. A protective plate surrounding the keyhole of a door, a light switch, etc.; or a flange on a pipe used to cover a hole in a floor or wall through which the pipe passes.

fan coil unit, furnace. The heat exchanger, fan and furnace portion of the HVAC system, which delivers the temperature-controlled air to the duct system; usually located in a closet or attic.

fascia, fasia. A flat horizontal member of a cornice placed in a vertical position.

footing. That portion of the foundation of a structure that transmits loads directly to the soil; may be the widened part of a wall or column, the spreading courses under a foundation wall, a foundation of a column, etc.; used to spread the load over a greater area to prevent or reduce settling.

foundation. Any portion of a structure that serves to support everything above it while it transmits the loads to the soil.

french drain. A drainage system consisting of slotted pipe placed in porous backfill which is used to collect ground water and transport it to another location.

furring. Thin wood or metal strips attached to a wall or ceiling to level the surface or extend the surface; usually covered with Sheetrock or plaster.

GFI. Abbreviation for ground fault interceptor; it is a circuit breaker required by code in areas where moisture may cause a shock hazard, such as the bathroom or garage.

girder. A large or principal beam used to support concentrated loads at isolated points along its length; in residential construction, it supports the floor or ceiling joists.

glue-laminated beam, timber. A manufactured product consisting of four or more wood layers bonded together with adhesive.

grade beam. That portion of the foundation system which supports the exterior wall of the superstructure or the slab; it may sit on a spread footing or bear directly on the soil.

head, header. Double wood pieces supporting joists in a floor or double wood members placed on edge over windows and doors to transfer the roof and floor weight to the studs.

honeycomb. Voids left in concrete due to failure of the mortar to effectively fill the spaces among the coarse aggregate particle.

HVAC. Abbreviation for heating, ventilation, and air-conditioning.

joist hanger. A metal strap or angle used to fix a joist to a girder or beam.

joists. Small rectangular sectional members arranged parallel from wall to wall in a building, or resting on beams or girders. Their function is to support the floor above or the ceiling below.

laminated beam. *See* glue-laminated beam.

lightweight concrete. Concrete of substantially lower density than normal concrete.

lintel. A structural horizontal member over an opening which is used to carry the weight of the wall above it.

percolation test. A test to determine the rate at which a particular soil absorbs effluent; a hole is dug in the soil and filled with water, then the rate at which the water level drops is measured.

pitch. The angle of the slope of the roof, usually expressed as a ratio of vertical rise to horizontal run.

post-tension cables. Multistrand high-strength steel wire used as reinforcing in concrete slabs and beams.

post-tensioning. A method of prestressing concrete by providing tension to the reinforcing cables after the concrete has set.

Proctor compaction test. A test to determine the optimum moisture content of a soil for compaction, or the percentage of soil compaction (density) achieved.

purlin. A horizontal member running across the rafters on which the roof deck or covering is placed.

rafter. one of a series of parallel structural roof members spanning from an exterior wall to a center ridge beam or ridge board.

rebar. *See* reinforcing bar.

reinforcing bar, steel. A steel bar used to strengthen concrete by providing additional strength in tension.

ridge beam, board. A thick longitudinal plank to which the upper ends of the rafters are attached for support and stability.

roofing felt. An asphalt-impregnated felt paper used under shingles as additional waterproofing.

screed. Firmly established grade strips or side forms for unformed concrete which will guide the strikeoff in producing the desired plane or shape.

sheathing. A covering (usually boards, plywood or wall boards) placed over exterior studding or rafters of a building; provides a base for the application of wall or roof cladding.

sill, sill plate, soleplate. A horizontal timber, at the bottom of the frame of a wood structure, which rests on the foundation.

slab. The upper part of a reinforced concrete floor, which is carried on grade beams below.

slump. A measure of the consistency of freshly mixed concrete, mortar or stucco; equal to the decrease in height , measured to the nearest inch of the molded mass immediately after its removal from the slump cone.

soffit. The exposed undersurface of any overhead component of a building, such as an arch, balcony, beam, cornice, lintel or vault.

standing seam. In metal roofing, a type of seam between adjacent sheets of material, made by turning up the edges of two adjacent sheets and then folding them over.

stirrup. A bent steel rod, usually U-shaped, used to tie or hold the main reinforcing bars in place, and also to add some additional reinforcing strength to the concrete.

subsurface investigation. The soil boring and sampling program, together with the associated laboratory tests, necessary to establish subsurface profiles and the relative strengths, compressibility and other characteristics of the various strata encountered within the depths likely to have an influence on the design (especially of the foundation) of the project.

top plate. The horizontal member at the top of the wall studs; on the top floor, the lower ends of the rafters are attached to it.

truss. A combination of structural members usually arranged in triangular units to form a rigid framework for spanning between load-bearing walls.

underpinning. The rebuilding or deepening of the foundation of an existing building to provide additional or improved support.

vapor barrier. A moisture-impervious layer or coating which prevents the passage of moisture or vapor into a structure.

wall tie. *See* brick tie.

welded wire mesh, fabric. A series of longitudinal and transverse wires arranged at right angles to each other and welded together at all points of intersection; used as reinforcing in concrete—usually sidewalks and driveways.

INDEX